Mo̶̶̶̶̶̶ 1892   ̶̶̶̶̶ 1891

Patsie 1936

Todd 1915

June 1934

Pearl 1916

Billie 1932

Virginia 1917

Johnnie 1931

Ruby 1918

Dick 1929

Opal 1920

Garnette 1928

Clyde 1925

Wilbur 1922

Our Family
is a circle of
strength and love.
With every birth the circle
grows. Every joy shared
adds more love. Every
crisis faced together
makes the circle
stronger.

12
+me

by Pat Likes

Hannibal Books
Hannibal, Missouri - "America's Hometown"

Use coupon in back to order extra copies of this and other books published by Hannibal Books.

Back Row, left to right, Clyde, Dad, Todd, Virginia,
Ruby, Wilbur, Pearl, Opal, Mom.
Front Row, left to right, Billie, Johnnie, Dick, June,
Garnette, Patsie.

*To my husband, Marvin J,
who ran the "gamut of emotions" with me as
the writing of "12 + me"
brought memories to life.*

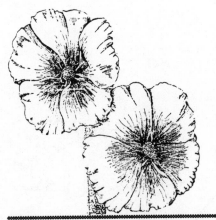

Table of Contents

Remembering 11

1 Pike County Patsie 15

2 Mom's Circle of Love 25

3 The Farm by the Shining River 41

4 My Sunshine Sister 47

5 Surviving 55

6 Sparrows in the Wedding Bed 65

7 The River 77

8 A Fizzled Fourth 85

9 Slick Blue 91

10 Mouse Pies and a Mystery 97

11 School's Not Always a "Cinch" 107

12 The Big Lesson 111

13 Miss Mundy Had a Way 121

14 Clyder, Sweet as Apple Cider 127

15 The Change in Dad's Pocket 137

Afterword/Appreciations 149

Mom's Recipes 153

INTRODUCTION

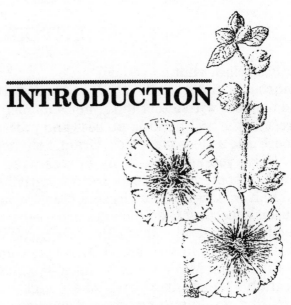

Remembering

"Grampat! Grampat! Come and see! The hollyhocks have flowers all over. We can make some dolls!"

I stepped quietly onto my kitchen porch. Four-year-old Hannah was standing amidst the tall, blossom covered hollyhock stalks, her tousled flaxen curls, bejeweled by the morning sun, offering dazzling competition to the delicate beauty of the flowers.

"Here's a pink one, Gram. We can make a pink doll. Pink is for girls. We can't make one for Dylan 'cause there's no blue ones and blue is for boys."

I allowed myself a moment to savor the scene before granting her request. Hollyhocks are special to me. I spent countless summer days of my childhood playing in the shade of tall hollyhock stalks. They bordered the front yard of my childhood home and now our new country home in rural west central Illinois has afforded me the space to indulge in a little nostalgia. And it has allowed my grandchildren to touch a part of my past.

"C'mon, Gram. Show me how to make hollyhock dolls like you did when you were a little girl, ple-e-ease." I walked down the steps and over to the familiar scene. I snapped Hannah's chosen pink blossom from the stalk. "Oh, Gram, isn't it beautiful? Now what do you do?"

I pinched a bud from the stalk and attached it to the stem of the blossom with a toothpick. For a moment, Hannah lost interest in the doll-making process and pressed her inquisitive nose into a blossom. "Yuck, Gram, hollyhocks don't smell good. Here, you smell it." Tiny fingers wrestled a maroon-colored blossom from the stalk and shoved it against my nose.

Hannah was right. The blossom didn't "smell good" if one had been expecting the redolence of expensive perfume, but it smelled good to me. It smelled of my childhood on a 300 acre tenant farm in western Illinois just across the Mississippi River from Mark Twain's Hannibal, Missouri

Hannah's encounter with the "yucky" blossom had transported me to another time, a long ago time when my world was warm summer sun and hollyhock shade and a white farmhouse teeming with activity. The six room, two-story, clapboard house, with its two screened-in porches, nestled comfortably on a thick lawn of bluegrass beneath cottonwood and maple trees and a magnificent old sycamore. The timbers of my home were not threaded with electrical wiring — the yellow glow of kerosene lamps warmed nighttime windows. Water did not run magically from chrome faucets — a bucket, filled fresh every morning at the livestock watering pump, held a day's supply of drinking water. The "bathroom" stood just beyond the border of the northwest corner of the yard.

It was in this house that I first sang "You Get a Line and I'll Get a Pole" with my curly-haired brother Clyde. It was from this haven that I ventured out into the lush green yard and watched though the pickets of our front yard gate as my sister, June, and the three youngest boys chased Slick Blue, the infamous bird eating tomcat.

It was from this yard that a little six-year-old with braided hair ran through that picket gate and down the lane to Smith School. Mr. Drusen, Miss Kathryn, and Mrs. Mundy, each in their own way, became a forever part of my life.

"Gram!" Hannah stamped an impatient little foot on the moist ground, bringing my attention back to the job at hand.

"Are you gonna finish my doll, or not?"

I completed the doll, and I made a promise to myself. I decided that one day I would write down the hollyhock memories. I would tell Hannah and Dylan about their six great-aunts and their six great-uncles and their Great-Grandma and Great-Grandpa Dunker.

So this chronicle is for you, Hannah, and for you, Dylan. Maybe it will help you to know just who "Grampat" really is.

Chapter 1

Pike County Patsie

"Here's Huck Finn; he ain't got no family. What you going to do 'bout him?"

"Adventures of Huckleberry Finn"

"Look," my sister, June, said pointing to the calendar hanging on our kitchen wall. "Right here it says 'June, 1943' and June's my name; it's on the calendar. That makes me famous. Your name's not on the calendar, Pat. Sorreee," she sang. June tossed me a smug little smile and accepted brother Bill's invitation to go horseback riding.

I was only two years younger than June, but to an almost seven year old, a nine year old is almost a grown up and very wise.

I threw myself against my mother's legs. "Mom!" I wailed, "why isn't my name on the calendar? How come I'm not famous?"

"Why, Patsie Ellen, you are famous. You're our own little 'Pike County Patsie.' You don't have to have your name on the calendar to be famous. Anyway, June Charlene was named for your dad. Since his name is Charles, I named her Charlene."

I wailed even louder. Not only was June's name on the calendar, she was named for Dad.

"I'll tell you what. Since your birthday is in July how would you like for me to call you Julie? It sounds like July." I quit crying and dried my tears on her apron. That sounded better than nothing.

I crawled up on my tall stool by the kitchen table. Mom turned a great bowl of bread dough onto its oil-cloth covered surface and began kneading. Nearly every other day Mom baked six to nine loaves of bread (depending on whether or not company was due), and today was baking day. Quick hands, all too familiar with this ritual, deftly formed smooth loaves from the mound of dough. I pinched a piece of dough from the first plump loaf.

"Patsie Ellen," Mom laughed, "now that loaf will have a dimple in it."

"Tell me about the other kids' names, Mom." I loved to sit on my stool by the kitchen table and listen to Mom tell me why she gave my twelve brothers and sisters the names they had and where she and Dad lived when each of us was born. Not only did she include the name of the country doctor who delivered each of us, she even remembered just exactly what every one of us weighed and the times of our births.

"Let's see, now," Mom began, "Todd, whose given name is Charles Franklin, was named for your dad and your Uncle Frank."

"Why do you call him, 'Todd' if his name is Charles?"

"When Pearl was learning to talk, she couldn't say Charlie; she said something that sounded like 'Toddy' so we shortened it to Todd and we've called him that ever since."

"How about Pearl? Is her name different than 'Pearl?'"

"No, but she did call Virginia 'Birdie' because she couldn't say Virginia. She and Virginia are named for friends. Ruby was named for my baby sister, your Aunt Ruby. Opal was named for a friend."

"You sure must've had lots of friends."

Mom laughed, "I guess we did because Clyde and Wilbur were named after friends, too."

"But Garnette Isabelle was named for my cousin Garnette and my Grandma Dunker, Clara Isabelle, wasn't she?" Garnette was closer to my age so I felt more knowledgeable about her. "And Dick was named Richard Frederick — 'Frederick' was my Grandpa Dunker's first name. Johnnie's whole name is John Stanley; 'John' is for Uncle John." I was on familiar ground now. Garnette, Dick, John, Bill, and June were close to me in age so it was easier to remember things about them. "Bill is William Burnell 'cause we had a Great Uncle William Dunker and June Charlene thinks she's smart 'cause she's named after Dad."

"Now, Patsy, June didn't choose her name; your Dad and I did."

It doesn't matter who named her, I thought to myself, *she still thinks she's smart because she's named after Dad.* I didn't pursue the matter any further, because I didn't want Mom to get aggravated with me. Instead, I wanted her to tell me about my arrival into the family.

"Tell me about the day I came to live here." I settled in. This was my favorite story.

"You came to live with us on July 9th, 1936 at ten o'clock in the evening. The weather was very hot, a hundred degrees and above every day, and that day was no different. It was an awful dry year, too, and our crops were terrible.

"Heat or no heat, you arrived. Dr. Ailshire and Mrs. Robbins were here. I'll never forget Dr. Ailshire saying, 'Her eyes are like chunks of coal, Mrs. Dunker; just see how big and black they are. This is a fine baby.' I was so proud of you. Your Dad chose your first name and I named you Ellen, after Mrs. Robbins. She was such a sweet lady.

"All of you kids were born in Illinois, but you're the only one the stork brought to live with us here in Pike County. All the older kids down to Johnnie were born in Mason County, and Johnnie, Billie, and June were born in Peoria County."

Mom plopped two more loaves of bread dough into the pan. Before she could start listing our birth weights, my pet kitten ambled across the floor from the south kitchen porch.

"Patsie, I wish you'd take your kitten outside. I'm working

in bread dough." I jumped down from my stool and picked up the kitten, carrying him across the screened-in kitchen porch and out into the back yard.

As I stepped outside, June and Bill came dashing up on their horses. I raced out to meet them.

"Guess what? My name is on the calendar. My name is Julie now, Julie for July."

Bill laughed. "It is not; it's Patsie. C'mon June, let's water our horses before we go back out."

Cradling my kitten in my arms, I moped back to the kitchen porch and climbed into the swing. *June and Bill seem so happy,* I thought. *Why shouldn't they be? June was named for a month and for Dad and Bill was named for a great-uncle. Everybody in my family has a special reason for their name but me. Oh, I was named Ellen after Ellen Robbins, who came over the night I arrived, but she wasn't a relative or a special friend; she was just a neighbor.*

The names of all my brothers and sisters began to fill my mind. Todd, Pearl, Virginia, Ruby, Opal, Wilbur, Clyde, Garnette, and Dick were born in Mason County, and Johnnie, Bill, and June were born in Peoria County. One fact soon became obvious; I was the only one of Mom and Dad's 13 kids who came to live with them after their move to Pike County; Mom had made that very clear by calling me "Pike County Patsie."

And then the thought struck me: *I'm adopted! That's why June has such a special name; she's their last baby. When Mom and Dad moved to Pike County they probably found me some place and just brought me home with them and then went to Dr. Ailshire's office and signed some papers to keep me. Maybe even Dr. Ailshire gave me to them or maybe Mrs. Robbins found me and brought me here.*

My over-active imagination ran wild. I didn't consider that parents who already had twelve children would not be particularly interested in adopting another .

But Mom always said I was such a cute little baby, my mind raced. *Maybe I was so cute that they couldn't stand to leave me; maybe they just felt sorry for me because my real mom and dad didn't want me.*

And what about Aunt Sarah? I reminded myself. *Mom's sister, Aunt Sarah, wanted me. She tried to take me home with her. Aunt Sarah said that Mom didn't need anymore kids to raise. She made Uncle John drive her all the way down to Pike County so she could get me.*

Mom had told me that story lots of times. She said that when I was just a few weeks old, Aunt Sarah, Uncle John and their daughter, Mable, came down to see me. They lived near Mason City, and it was a long trip.

Almost every time Mom would tell me about when I came to live with her and Dad she would add: "Your Aunt Sarah said, 'Cora, you have too much work on your hands. I'll take the new baby and care for her.' But I wouldn't have any part of such an idea." Mom was adamant about that. She and Aunt Sarah had a falling out about it, but only for a little while.

Thinking back on the story set me to wondering; maybe they did something like draw straws for me and Mom won. How could I find the truth?

The writing desk. I just knew I could find the answer in the writing desk because Mom and Dad kept all their important papers there. If adoption papers existed, they would be found in the writing desk. But this solution offered a major problem. Nobody, and I mean nobody, got into that desk unless either Mom or Dad requested it. However, considering the seriousness of my predicament, I decided to risk it.

I left my cat sleeping on the swing and slipped into the living room from the front porch. I tiptoed across the cool, linoleum covered floor to the writing desk. I was sure it held more secrets than any other place in the whole house, because it was such a forbidden place to us kids.

I pulled the ornately carved oak lid down. Secured by two flat brass hinges, one on each side, the lid created a perfect writing surface and exposed wonderfully intricate slots and tiny drawers just waiting to be explored.

Since this was the summer of my seventh year, I could read well enough to recognize the word "Ledger" on the big gray book in which Dad kept his farm accounts. He stored it in a tall slot on the right side of the desk.

I knew that Mom kept an extra writing tablet and en-velopes in the small drawer next to the ledger slot, but I didn't know what else she might have kept there. I pulled that drawer open.

I had to be quiet because Mom was still in the next room washing up the baking things. I sure didn't want her to know what I was doing. I hoped she thought I was still out in the porch swing with my cat. I was feeling guilty about snooping in the writing desk, but my need to know whether or not I was adopted was all-consuming.

The contents of the drawer were not particularly interest-ing. Besides the writing tablet, it held some letters from Aunt Sarah and a picture of Dad when he was a little boy. All very familiar items.

The space under the center drawer held intriguing little rolled documents tied with red ribbons. I unrolled some of these only to find Mom and Dad's marriage license and some of our Sunday school and public school certificates — again familiar items and none of which answered my question.

I didn't know for sure what I was looking for, but I was sure I would recognize the word "adopted" when I saw it. The center drawer held some papers which I didn't understand, but since none of them offered "the word," I closed that drawer and began to check the left side of the desk.

The slot on that side held a BIG CHIEF school tablet, a few pencils, Mom's everyday writing tablet, a fountain pen and a bottle of ink. Nothing there that solved my mystery.

The small drawer just next to the far left slot was the last bastion of secrecy. I couldn't recall ever seeing that drawer opened. Somehow, when Mom and Dad asked me to bring them something from the desk, it was never contained in that drawer.

I had to hurry. June and Bill would soon be in for dinner, and if either of them caught me rummaging through the writing desk, they'd tell Mom, or even worse, they'd tell Dad.

I opened the little drawer. Some business envelopes ad-dressed to Dad appeared to be all it held until I saw the corner of something else. I picked up the envelopes and there alone in the drawer lay a tiny white box only slightly larger than a penny match box.

I had never seen this box before. I opened it and felt a smooth puff of cotton. I lifted the cotton, and to my horror, an eye resting on a second piece of cotton stared back at me.

Hurriedly I shoved the box back into the drawer and withdrew my hand in fright. My heart pounded. Cautiously, I looked back into the drawer, fearful of what I might see. The contents of the box were scattered. The two pieces of cotton were in one corner and the box lay on its edge in another corner. As if moved by some unseen force, the upside down eye rocked noiselessly inside the lid of the tiny box.

I started toward the kitchen, but I was afraid of what might happen to the eye if I left the room. Rooted to the spot, I yelled. "Mom! Mom! Come quick! Look what I found; it's an eye! What is it? Is it somebody's?"

Mom hurried into the living room. "What's wrong? What's wrong?" she asked, wiping bread dough and flour from her hands onto her apron. Then she saw the opened drawer and its disheveled contents. She said nothing as she placed cotton over the eye and covered the box with its lid. Then she put the box back in the drawer, covered it with the envelopes, gently closed the drawer, and lifted the desk top back to its closed position.

"Patsie Ellen," she gently scolded, "what were you doing in the desk? Did someone ask you to get something from here?"

"No, I was just..."

She sat down on the chair next to the desk and pulled me onto her lap. "Honey, that eye belongs to your Dad. It's his extra glass eye. I'm sorry it scared you. I just didn't give any thought to the fact that you didn't know about it.

"You see, when your Dad was 12 years old, about the age Dickie is right now, a piece of steel flew into his eye and cut it very badly. The doctors took out the bad eye and replaced it with a glass eye. Your Aunt Sophia always said that your big brown eyes are just like your Dad's were before he had the accident."

The words rang in my ears — big brown eyes just like my Dad! *Then I can't be adopted. I am my Daddy's little girl!*

"...And so, Patsie Ellen," Mom was saying to me, "I know you were scared by what you found, and I'm sorry for that, but I hope you have learned not to get into this desk without permission."

I had learned, all right, but what I had learned had nothing to do with disobeying the rule about the desk; I had learned that I was not adopted.

Just then June and Bill walked into the kitchen. "Mom, where are you? Is dinner ready?"

I ran up to them, a satisfied grin on my round little face. "My name is 'Pike County Patsie' and it's not on the calendar and I don't care and Aunt Sophia says that my eyes are just like my Dad's." I danced around the kitchen table singing my story to them. Bill and June just looked at each other and laughed.

I don't recall ever checking closely to determine which of Dad's eyes was artificial. It didn't really matter, because from then on, whenever my Dad looked at me, his brown eyes told me that I was his "Pike County Patsie."

Years later, when I was making wedding plans, I mentioned to Dad that I had received some important documents with the name "Patricia" on them. As we visited over a cup of coffee, I asked, "Dad, do you think I should have that changed to Patsy, spelled P-a-t-s-y? I know that years ago everyone spelled my name P-a-t-s-i-e, but I don't spell it that way anymore."

"Why change it?" he asked. "I named you Patricia and your mother named you Ellen — Patricia Ellen Dunker, our only Pike County baby."

"But Dad," I protested, "My birth certificate states that my name is Patsie Ellen, spelled P-a-t-s-i-e."

"I told Virginia that we would name you Patricia, but we would probably call you Patsie and spell it P-a-t-s-i-e. I just bet when she told old Doc Ailshire your name, he got mixed up and wrote down Patsie Ellen instead of Patricia Ellen. I don't know when the spelling got changed to P-a-t-s-y." Dad laughed. "That's something — and all this time I thought I had a daughter named Patricia."

I didn't change my name, but I did add "Likes" to it. I am now and always shall be, Patsy Ellen Dunker Likes, nee "Pike County Patsie."

Chapter 2

Mom's Circle of Love

There is nothing comparable to the endurance of a woman.

"Mark Twain's Autobiography"

Mom was a lady. She always wore a starched print house dress covered with an equally starched print apron. After the birth of Garnette, her eighth child, Mom's weight gradually began to increase. By the time I arrived, her five-foot-four inch frame carried about one hundred and fifty pounds, but Mom was never fat. Her proud regal carriage defied the few extra pounds to detract from her pleasing appearance.

Although Mom and Dad had only fourth grade educations, they were particular about the way they talked. Potatoes, not "taters," grew in our garden. My worst offense to Mom's ear was "Ah will." Mom had only to look at me and ask, "Who will?" "I will," came my immediate reply.

When she was raising her family, Mom had few clothes. Other than her house dresses, she had only a dress to wear into town and a dress-up dress. When I was six, Dad bought her a navy blue gabardine suit and a soft pink blouse as special gifts for her fiftieth birthday, and when she wore them, she was the most beautiful mother in the world.

Mom would never answer the door in her bare feet. She made sure that my doll was dressed before I presented it to a guest. She always referred to Dad's prize bull as a "gentleman cow" and her trips to the outdoor toilet were made in almost complete secrecy. But she was not a prude.

Her paternal grandparents hailed from Ireland, and this daughter of a first generation Irish-American could dance an Irish jig with the best of them. I used to try to imitate her, but my fat little feet would not cooperate. When Uncle Frank's fiddle began to play a lively tune, Mom couldn't stand still. A just-slightly-below-the-calf length house dress was lifted a polite inch or so, freeing nimble feet to fly in perfect time with the music. Mom loved to dance.

My parents met at a square dance in the home of friends. Mom was twenty and she was beautiful. Her clear blue eyes sparkled with a tiny glint of mischief. She wore her chestnut brown hair in the Gibson Girl style and anchored it with a wide bow in the back. She had a perfect figure. Her bosom was just full enough and her hips just round enough, and she had a tiny waist around which Dad's arm fit perfectly as he danced into her life.

Aunt Sophia, Dad's oldest sister, insisted that Mom and Dad were always the handsomest couple on any dance floor. He wasn't a big man; he stood about five feet nine inches tall with dark wavy hair, but Dad's strong broad shoulders and trim body exuded pride and confidence.

"I met your dad at a square dance," Mom would tell us kids. "By the time he got up courage enough to ask me to dance, the only space left on the floor was in front of the cookstove, and I've been dancing there ever since."

Dad would interrupt, "Now, Corrie, it wasn't all my idea. You're the one who needed a ride home that night. And when I took you home, you tried to talk me into staying at your house later than I should.

"Why, when we started going out on a regular basis, you always hated to see me leave. Every time I brought you home from a dance you'd say, 'You don't have to leave just yet,

Charlie. We can sit here on the porch swing for awhile.'
Many's the night your Papa called out the door, 'Corrie, let
that poor boy go home.'"

"Charlie Dunker!" Mom would retort with a loving chuckle
in her voice. "You know better than that. The truth is, Papa
was hoping you'd go home so he wouldn't have to give that
little milk cow to me for my dowry. Poor man, with five
daughters, he finally ran out of milk cows."

I'll never know for sure who was shading the truth. I do
know that Mom and Dad loved and respected each other. It
was obvious in that certain look they exchanged. It was
evident in those pre-dawn summer walks they took to the
fishing pond. They caught a few fish, but they also caught a
few rare moments of quiet time before morning chores and
breakfast for a houseful of kids.

Mom was Dad's right hand. Although he was the bread-
winner, he depended on her for advice and support. And she
was the family worrier. "I never got too concerned about any
of you kids when you were sick unless your mother became
uneasy," Dad often said. "All she had to say was, 'Charlie, I
think they're gonna be fine' and I would go on about my work
and leave the worrying up to her."

We used to laugh and say that Mom was happy only when
she had something to worry about. So we supplied her with
a never ending worry list: from childhood illnesses, to playing
on the ice jam on the Mississippi River, to breaking young
colts for riding, to dating and staying out late, to families of
our own. Mom worried and her 13 children thrived.

A major concern for her at the onset of the winter of '35 - '36
was the knowledge that Opal and Ruby needed winter coats.
Mom had raised ducks during the summer before the move
to Pike County. She sold them just before the move and gave
the money to the girls for coats, but it wasn't enough.

One day, when she and Dad were driving their Model A
Ford over the bridge to Hannibal, she confided this worry to
him.

"I don't know what we can do about it, Corrie. We just don't
have any extra money."

"I know, I know," Mom agreed, but she couldn't get the coats off her mind. Dad parked in front of the grocery store. Mom stepped out of the truck and onto the sidewalk. As Dad came around the front of the truck, he saw her stomp one foot over something on the side walk. She stood perfectly still and stared straight ahead at a man who was walking toward them.

"What in the world is wrong with you?" Dad asked. The stranger walked on by. "What're you holding your foot on?"

"Did you think that man seemed to be looking for anything, Charlie?" she asked Dad.

"No, I guess not." Dad was more puzzled than ever.

Mom stooped and retrieved what appeared to be a slip of paper from beneath her shoe. "Good," she replied, "then I guess this twenty dollar bill is ours." Mom smiled as she handed Dad the money. "Now Opal and Ruby will have their new coats."

Aside from us kids, storms were a good source of worry material for Mom. Late-night spring thunderstorms sent her scurrying to the foot of the stairs ordering: "You kids get downstairs right now. A storm's comin' up". Sleepy headed little Dunkers from toddlers to teens came tumbling down the stairs at her command.

Any attempt to weather a spring storm in the comfort of our upstairs bedrooms was useless. If we weren't down the stairs and into the living room on the first call, Mom flew up the stairs with all the fluff and bother of a mother hen caring for newly hatched chicks. Much to her chagrin, though, Dad slept through most spring thunderstorms.

Nighttime winter winds also caused her much anxiety. I think they worried Dad, too. But she wouldn't trust anybody's watch over the Warm Morning coal stove in the living room except herself. "You go on to bed, Charlie," Mom would gently order, "I'll stay up and watch the stove for awhile."

The Warm Morning stove squatted along the north wall in the living room and served as our central heating system. A four-legged cast iron frame supported its three-foot cylindrical sheet-metal body, holding it about eight inches off the floor. A small door in the front of the frame allowed for easy removal of ashes, and a cast iron cap with a drop-down front opening door topped the stove. Mom always felt that Dad put entirely too much coal through this door when he banked the stove for the night. The tin stovepipe, which led from the back of the stove to a hole in the brick flue, sometimes glowed with a hint of red. When this happened, our stove watcher immediately adjusted the damper to allow only a minimal flow of air through the pipe and on out the flue.

When she felt that the fire had reached a comfortable level, Mom adjusted the damper one more time. She possessed an almost innate understanding of that damper. She knew that if it was closed completely, the stove would "puff" and coal smoke would find its way through the stove's lid and into the living room. And so she situated the damper at just the right angle, allowing no sparks to escape into the old brick flue. Then she went to bed.

I have to confess that I did derive a certain amount of comfort from her stove tending. And I have to admit that I took it all for granted.

I never wondered at the source of all that strength. Mom knew. Her Bible told her that there was a Higher Power keeping vigil over all of us. Oh, she and Dad supported, comforted, and loved each other, but Mom's inner strength came from her Bible.

I loved to sit on the cot in the living room, reading or listening to the radio, and peek at her reading the Bible. At the end of each day, Mom sat in her chair beside the lamp table and combed her long brown hair (it never did turn gray). Then she rested her five-and-dime reading glasses on her nose and picked up her Bible.

After only a few verses, her head began to nod and the Bible started sliding down her apron. "Mom," one of us would call, "you're falling asleep."

Startled, she would jump and reply, "Oh, I'm just resting my eyes." Then the reading began again. Even though the need for rest finally won out, a thorough knowledge and love of the Bible sustained her. Spiritual strength, gained from

spending those few minutes each evening with her Bible,
carried my gentle mother along a quiet, loving journey
through life. The sight of Mom reading the scripture in her
chair will remain with me forever.

I don't want to mislead you. We were not model children
during our growing up years, and often our house was anything but quiet — it's just that Mom handled it in a quiet
way. For the most part, anyway, she stayed in control.

She did have a proverbial Irish temper and it did flash now
and then. She was known to tie an unruly kid to the clothes-
line. And a bucket of water was emptied over the head of a
son who thought holding his breath would help him get his
way. But there were the times when threats of punishment
led to a merry chase around the kitchen table, with mother
and child collapsing onto the floor in a bundle of laughter,
and hugs and kisses settled the issue.

She could also get pretty aggravated with Dad. Like the
time he asked her if she'd like to ride over to Barry, Illinois
with him. Dad also invited Happy Loving to come along —
our Dutch neighbor whose round, bright blue eyes always
betrayed a kind of gentle deviltry.

Dad and Happy had two commonalties: both farmed and
both enjoyed a substantial sip of whiskey when a special
occasion demanded it. Such a time came on the morning Dad
and Mom drove to Barry.

Mom wasn't exactly pleased that their neighbor was going
along, because she knew what could happen when Dad and
Happy got together. Nevertheless, she climbed into the truck
with Dad, and they bounced down the lane to pick up Happy.

"Charlie, you can drop me off at Ownby's Store when we
get to Barry. I should be ready to go about noon. I'll be waiting
in front of the store."

Dad and Happy stopped at the door and Happy helped Mom
out of the truck. "I'm going to go see about some calves. I think
I can make a pretty good trade," Dad said to her.

The morning ran as scheduled. Mom completed her shopping and Dad picked her up at the set time. However, the
completion of the trade for the two calves had seemed just

the right occasion for Dad and Happy to make a stop at the local tavern before picking up their passenger. Mom knew where the two had been the minute Happy stepped out of the truck and offered the slightly aggravated passenger her place on the seat next to Dad.

Happy's usual jovial mien was a little too jovial, and Dad's ordinarily staid bearing had taken on more relaxation than normal. Still, the trip home was not unpleasant. Dad and Happy laughed and talked, and when they felt the story befit the lady in their midst, they relayed some local gossip to Mom. The need to strengthen a particular point in a story induced Happy to give Mom an occasional cuff on the shoulder. My indignant mother became increasingly irritated with such familiarity. With each thump on the shoulder, Mom moved closer to Dad.

When they reached the railroad tracks about four miles from home, Dad yelled, "Hang on!" He was having trouble keeping control of his '39 Ford pickup truck. New gravel on the descending side of the railroad crossing pulled the truck dangerously close to the edge of the road. A five-foot drop was imminent.

Plop! The truck bumped against a weed and grass covered ditch bank and tilted, causing Dad's door to be jammed against the bank and Happy to fall against Mom.

"Happy Loving, get off me and get out of this truck!" Mom's indignation at having any man except Dad at that proximity provided the extra physical strength needed to boost the robust Dutchman toward his door.

Mom left her packages in the truck and, with Dad and Happy, started walking the remaining four miles to our house. A neighbor picked them up before they had gone very far. He dropped Mom and Dad off and took Happy on home.

"Now, Charlie Dunker," Mom ordered as they came into the kitchen, "don't you ever invite Happy Loving to go to town with us again if you two intend to stop and drink."

Mom hung her coat in the kitchen closet and pulled her apron over her shopping dress. "I didn't like it one bit having that man squeezed against me like that! Humph!"

Dad laughed and headed for the shed to get the tractor. His embarrassed and proper wife swished her apron and reached for the skillets. "I'm going to fix dinner now. When you and the boys get back with the truck, we'll eat." Mom was back in control.

There were a few times in my life, though, when I thought reason totally left her — a very few, but it did happen. For example, there was the time when we had visitors from Missouri.

No matter how much we had to do, Mom was never too busy to keep clean beds. So when these almost forgotten acquaintances from Missouri drove up for a surprise three-day visit, Mom spread crisp white sheets on the bed in the upstairs spare room and welcomed them into our home. However, their habits of personal cleanliness were noticeably absent.

We didn't have a bath room — we didn't even have a pump in the kitchen until I was about six or seven. Depending on the weather, weekly baths were given to the little kids in the kitchen or on the two screened-in porches, boys on one — girls on the other. The older kids bathed in their rooms and hired men "washed up" either in the wash house or at the outside pump. My brothers, Clyde and Wilbur, built a barrel shower out behind the wash house. It was a seasonal bathing facility. They filled the barrel early in the morning and relied on solar power to heat their evening bath water.

Mom's nose soon recognized that our Missouri guests were not availing themselves of any of our bathing facilities. "Charlie, I don't know what I'm going to do. That mother is just plain lazy. She doesn't keep her baby clean at all." Mom began to worry. She was too polite to ask her guests to leave.

"They'll be leaving soon," Dad tried to console her. "At least they don't have bed bugs." Dad had no idea how wrong he was.

At last the worrisome guests departed. Mom filled a scrub bucket with water and foul smelling disinfectant and headed upstairs for the spare room.

I was sitting in the sycamore tree swing when the mattress landed right next to me. Mom had shoved it from an upstairs bedroom window. Marching around the corner of the house with a can of kerosene in one hand and a box of matches in the other, she headed for the mattress.

"Patsie," Mom ordered, "get out of the way. I'm gonna burn this mattress."

"Don't, Mom," I cried, "You'll burn my tree down and I won't have any place for my swing." Mom would have burned the mattress right then and there, but Dad came around the corner of the house calling to her.

"What in the world are you doing, Corrie?"

"I'm gonna burn this mattress. It's full of bedbugs. I told you those people were dirty."

"Here, let's get it out from under the tree." Dad knew it would do no good to argue with her. He grabbed the mattress and the two of them pulled it out by the garden where Mom doused it with kerosene and set it ablaze.

I ran in the house to get away from the smoke and to see what she did to the spare room. If Mom would burn a mattress just because of a little bug or two, it was hard to tell what she might do to a whole room. I ran up the stairs imagining all sorts of things. In the middle of the bedroom, I saw the naked old iron bed — each leg standing in a tin can of kerosene.

Mom was death on bugs. A few years earlier she burned a pie cupboard. A neighbor lady bought eggs from Mom. She wore the same dress and sunbonnet for days, sometimes more than a week at a time, and she chewed tobacco. On egg day, this neighbor would invite herself into the kitchen and thump her egg basket onto the top of the pie cupboard. Then she'd seat herself at the kitchen table and wouldn't budge until Mom offered her a cup of coffee.

After a few weeks of these uninvited visits, Mom found roaches in her pie cupboard. She immediately emptied the shelves of their contents and singlehandedly pushed the cupboard through the kitchen door to the edge of the porch and then tossed it into the backyard. It met with the same demise as the mattress. Mom quit selling eggs to the neighbor lady.

Our house was never totally spotless, but along with her attitude about our beds, Mom was very particular about her kitchen. My sister, Garnette — eight years older than me — was Mom's kitchen helper when I was small, but she didn't always share Mom's attention to detail. One particular early summer day, when I was almost two and Garnette was ten, Mom put me under the care of this big sister while she started dinner for the men in the fields. Dad came home mid-morning and announced that extra men would be at the dinner table.

"Garnette, run to the garden and bring in some swiss-chard and spinach," Mom directed. "I'll put some ham on to cook." Garnette, who was enjoying a story-time with me and hated gathering garden vegetables, stomped off and yanked tender greens from the patch. A quick splash under the pump and a careless once-over for bugs found the greens bubbling in the ham pot before Mom got a chance to check them.

"Set this bowl of cottage cheese on the table, Garnette, and make sure the bread and butter are on." Garnette obliged and a bowl of cottage cheese found its way to the table along with green onions, bread and butter, and apple butter.

"There, now," Mom said, surveying the noon offering, "as soon as those greens and ham get done dinner will be ready." Turning to Garnette she asked, "Did you look the greens closely?" (In Mom's kitchen, "looking" the leafy vegetables from the garden meant checking them thoroughly for bugs and worms and then washing them at least twice.)

"Yes," Garnette answered a little sheepishly.

Mom lifted the lid from the steaming pot. "Oh, no, Garnette! You didn't look the greens!" Three swollen worms floated atop the bubbling pot. "Open the door," Mom demanded. She grabbed up the pot of ham and greens. "I'm gonna feed this mess to the chickens."

Mom hurried to the chicken yard and tossed out the greens, ham and all. "Now, you wash this pan," Mom admonished Garnette when she came back into the kitchen. I'll slice some more ham and fix some gravy. That'll have to do for our dinner. Nothing more was said of the incident, but Garnette learned never to bring anything unwashed and "unlooked" into Mom's kitchen.

Crucial to our well being and to the quality of our food was the care of the milk that Dad and the boys brought in twice daily. Milk buckets were washed after each use in soapy hot water, and whenever possible, set out in the sun to dry. Milk storage crocks and jars and the big hand-cranked machine that separated the cream from the milk met with the same cleaning treatment.

Dad and the boys were in charge of milking the cows and separating the milk. Once in awhile I followed them to the barn. I held my tin cup under the cow's udder while Dad's quick hands rhythmically coaxed the warm milk into the waiting cup. Then I perched on an extra milking stool and drank the foamy warm nourishment while I watched the kittens who lived in the barn. They drank the early morning milk, too, clustering just close enough to the cows to miss an occasional kick. Holding their heads erect with an affected attitude of indifference, they vied for jet streams of milk deftly squirted in their direction by the youthful milkers in the barn. When their faces finally dripped with too much of the inaccurately aimed morning offering, the haughty little creatures retired to the back of the barn to clean themselves. They conducted this ritual with such an air of propriety that even Dad stopped to watch and laugh.

When the milking was done, Dad and the boys brought it into the kitchen and poured it into the separator. Dad turned the crank as thick sweet cream poured softly into a crock from one spout, and blue-white skimmed milk danced noisily into the milk bucket from the other spout, raising a mound of bubbly foam.

Often, we danced precariously around the bubbly milk, daring Dad to catch us and push our faces into the mounting foam. Disappointment came only when we were too lithesome for Dad's quick grasp and missed out on the dunking.

Most mornings, one three-gallon bucket of whole milk was saved back for table use and cooking. When Dad and the boys finished separating the milk, it became Mom's responsibility, and she didn't take it lightly. I've often wondered if my mother hailed from a long line of Irish milk maids and the knowledge was inherent. She knew exactly how to care for milk.

Before Mom could give what she considered proper care to the milk, she cleared off the breakfast table and washed up the dishes. Then the oil cloth covering on the kitchen table met with a thorough scrubbing. Only after these chores were completed would Mom begin the "handling" of the milk.

She poured the whole milk into sterilized crocks, covered them with dinner plates, and set them in the ice box to chill. Gallon jars filled with milk were often hung from the ends of ropes down into the well. The method of chilling depended on the availability of ice. Cream was chilled in the same manner, to be churned into butter later that day or the next.

Mom usually poured some of the skimmed milk into a gallon crock and set it back to clabber for cottage cheese. She set the rest of it on the back porch for Dad to pour over oats and feed to the hogs.

Having dispensed with all the milk, cleanup time was next. My Irish milkmaid mother reveled in this part of the job. Music and soap bubbles floated and bounced through the kitchen as the scrubbed and sterilized milk utensils left her dishpan.

I loved it. I especially loved being six years old and having time to spend with Mom while all the rest of the kids were in school. Every morning I pulled my stool up to the kitchen table and visited or just sat contentedly and listened to her sing. My favorite songs were "Bringing in the Sheaves" and "Red Wing."

Sometimes I got a wooden spool, long before emptied of its sewing thread, and blew soap bubbles. I would rob Mom's dish pan of its softened wet soap and rub one end of the spool on the slippery surface. A gentle puff of air through the other end sent a cascade of bubbles across the kitchen.

And sometimes Mom would let me get her jewelry box and play with the treasures stored inside — a couple of brooches, a wide, thin wedding band, and a gold bracelet.

The brooches were gifts from the older kids. Shortly after Garnette was born, the thin, worn wedding band had been removed from the once slender finger it had originally adorned. Loving hands, plumped from work and changes of age, had placed it in the jewelry box for safe keeping.

The bracelet was my favorite. Dad had given it to Mom on their wedding day. Its plain, yet elegant style was smooth to the touch and slipped easily over my little girl hand and wrist. Tiny, engraved, rose-tinted flowers graced the top of the oval-shaped tube of gold. A delicate hinge on one side and a miniature spring clasp on the other allowed the bracelet to open and then close securely around the wrist.

"Did Dad really buy the bracelet just for you?" Mom must have told me that story a hundred times, but I never tired of asking for it.

"Yes, Patsie Ellen, he did. He gave it to me the day we got married. I thought it was the most beautiful thing I'd ever seen in my whole life."

"Tell me about how you always wanted something gold and how Dad came to be the one to give it to you." On this occasion, I jumped down from the stool and got my doll. This story was too good to be missed by anyone.

"Well," Mom began, "When I was just a little older than you, probably eight years old, I saw an ad in a magazine. It said that if ten packages of garden seed were sold, the seller would receive a gold ring.

"I always wanted a piece of gold jewelry, so I begged Mama and Papa until they let me order the seeds. When the packages of seeds finally arrived, Papa let me ride into town with him so that I could sell them to the neighbors along the way. It didn't take me long to sell all of them.

"Then I ordered the ring. One day Papa came in with the package in his hand. 'Let's see now,' he said, 'I do believe there's a package here for little Corrie Petty.' He held it high in the air.

"'Oh, give it to her, Marion,' Mama said. 'She's waited long enough.' I opened the package and slipped the ring on my finger. It felt so good. I had never seen such a beautiful ring.

I wore it night and day."

I squeezed Mary Ellen, my doll. I knew the next part was going to be sad.

"A few days later, I noticed that my finger was sorta green around the ring. Soon the ring turned so green that I couldn't even tell it had ever been gold, and I couldn't polish it back to gold again. So I threw it away. I cried hard that night. Mama couldn't say anything that would make me stop. Finally I fell asleep.

"The next day Mama rode into town with Papa. It wasn't very long at all 'til I saw that team and wagon bouncing down our lane and home. Mama was all smiles when she got out of the wagon. 'I have a surprise for you, Corrie,' she said. And she handed me some new ribbons for my hair."

"Did you like them?" I asked, caressing my own long braids. I loved getting ribbons for my pigtails. I felt sure that Mom had enjoyed the new ribbons her mama had brought for her hair.

"Yes, I liked them, but I still wanted a gold ring. I didn't tell Mama that, though. I told Mama that I was glad to get the ribbons.

"Years went by, and I never got any more gold jewelry. Then one day when I became a grown-up girl, I met your Dad." Here Mom would always get a warm, far-away look in her eyes and she would stop talking for a minute.

"Did you like him a lot?"

"Yes, I liked your Dad a lot. I liked him so much that when he asked me to marry him I said 'yes.'"

"Is that when he gave you the bracelet?"

"No, not yet. I haven't gotten to that part yet." Mom carried separator parts out to the kitchen porch and hung them up to dry. "Now let's see, where was I?" she pondered, stepping back into the kitchen.

"You were coming to the part where Dad gave you the bracelet."

"Oh, yes. Well, my mama helped me make a pretty rose-colored wedding dress and Papa promised me one of his best milk cows for my dowry. Then the day came for our wedding."

"Here it comes, Mary Ellen," I whispered to my doll. "This is the part where Dad gives the bracelet to Mom."

"Just before we stood before the minister, your dad turned to me and said, 'Hold out your wrist. Corrie I have something for you.' And he fastened the gold bracelet around my wrist. Then we said our wedding vows, and he slipped the gold wedding band on my finger."

"You must've really been happy 'cause you got two gold jewelries that day." I squirmed with delight.

Mom laughed and emptied the last of the water used in washing the milk utensils. "Yes, I guess I was happy that day, and I was lucky, too, Patsie Ellen 'cause if I hadn't married your Dad, I wouldn't have you!"

When Mom died and we divided her things, all the girls said, "Well, we know for sure that all of Mom's jewelry goes to Pat." I agreed to serve only as the keeper of the jewelry — the gold bracelet and the thin, worn wedding band.

The precious bracelet encircled my wrist when I walked down the aisle as a bride. Thus began the tradition of the wedding bracelet. From that time on, Dunker granddaughters and great-granddaughters have worn the bracelet on their special day. The next one will be Virginia's granddaughter, Tresa, who will wed Dan Spencer, a minister's son from Alabama.

Between weddings, Mom's gold bracelet and wedding band lie in a pink velvet jewelry case on my dresser. From time to time I stop and look at her "jewelries." And each time I thank God for Mom's circle of love.

Chapter 3

The Farm by the Shining River

*All life demands change, variety, contrast, — else
there is small zest to it.*

"Mark Twain's Travels with Mr. Brown"

If Mom hadn't married Dad, she wouldn't have been in Pike County, Illinois, either. Pike County really wasn't Mom's choice of places to live, but she knew Dad felt good about the move, so she made no complaints.

When Louis Heckman, a prominent and respected businessman from Manito, Illinois, bought the 300-acre livestock-and-grain farm in Pike County, he knew who would operate it — my dad. Dad had operated a number of Peoria and Mason county farms for Mr. Heckman and had always brought them up to top production capabilities. Through the years, the two men had developed a landowner/operator arrangement with each farm Dad managed, which proved to be financially beneficial to both. So when the Pike County farm was offered, Dad didn't hesitate to accept it.

The 1935 move to Pike County was quite an adventure for the kids. The biggest stream they had ever lived by was a creek, and now they would be living within a stone's throw of the shining Mississippi River. Having moved many times, nobody felt threatened by the relocation to Pike County. They knew Dad would make a go of it. And Dad knew that Todd would be his right hand man. In order to facilitate the long process of restoring the farm, Todd came down earlier than the rest of the family.

Dad had bought an old Model T Ford for five dollars so that Todd would have something to drive down to the new farm. As soon as he got to Hull, Todd established credit with a local oil dealer, Addis Praul. "Well, young man," Mr. Praul said, "if Louis Heckman trusts your Dad enough to rent him that farm, then I guess I'll set up an account with you." Todd started working on the farm while he waited for Dad and Mom to join him.

On a warm August day in 1935, the rest of the family moved. Dad rented two stock trucks and loaded them with furniture, two crates of chickens, and Dunker kids. Clyde and Wilbur rode in the back of one of the trucks and Opal and Ruby rode in the other. Dad and Mom drove their Model A, bringing Garnette, Dick, Johnnie, Billie, and baby June. Pearl and Virginia had taken jobs in Peoria, Illinois, as maids, so they stayed behind.

It was mid-morning before the caravan began the four hour trip to their new home. During a filling station stop, the driver of the truck in which Clyde and Wilbur were riding, lit a cigarette. "Here, you boys want one?"

"Sure," Wilbur answered, reaching for the two cigarettes the man held toward him.

"Wilbur," Clyde whispered, "what'll Dad say?"

"It's all right, Clyde. I'm almost fourteen. I'm old enough to smoke."

Eleven-year-old Clyde laughed nervously. "I'm glad Dad's ahead of us in the Model A; I wouldn't want him to see us do this."

"Quit worryin', Clyde. He won't." As soon as the old stock truck rumbled off the station drive and onto the highway, Wilbur handed one of the cigarettes to Clyde. "Here," he directed, "put this in your mouth and I'll show you how to light it." Hovering against a mattress to keep the wind from blowing out their match, the boys lit their cigarettes.

Clyde began choking on the cigarette smoke. "Whew," he coughed, "I don't know what's so good about smokin'; I'm about to choke to death. I gotta get some air."

"It's fun. What's wrong?" Feigning a casual air, Wilbur put the cigarette to his lips and pulled the smoke into his lungs, but the action backfired on him. He strangled.

Choking and coughing, the two boys left their protected spot next to the mattress and came up for air. "Look out, Clyde, you've knocked the fire from my cigarette. Where'd it go?"

"I don't know, but mine's gone, too. It probably blew over the side of the truck. I'm gonna throw this thing away." Clyde tossed his cigarette out of the truck and sat back down.

"You've ruined mine, too, and I don't have anymore matches." Wilbur flipped the cigarette from his hand and joined Clyde. "These cigarettes must've been cheap. The guy that's drivin' our truck wouldn't give 'em to us if they had been good ones."

"My mouth tastes awful, Wilbur."

"Here, Mom put a jar of water in here for us. Take a drink." Both boys drank from the fruit jar of water and settled back for the remainder of the trip. But their reverie was short lived.

Clyde was the first to notice it. "Wilbur, I smell smoke. Did you light another cigarette?"

"No, but I smell it, too. Oh, no, Clyde, the mattress is on fire. The smoke's comin' from that corner next to you. Help me find the fire."

Space conservation had prompted the need to fold the old cotton bedding in half, and the pocket this created had caught the illusive cigarette fire. Following the trail of smoke, the boys found a smoldering fire in the crevice of the mattress. "Quick, Clyde. Give me the rest of that water. I can pour it on the fire and stop it from spreading." Wilbur succeeded in drowning the fire, but the mattress had a dinner-plate size charred area on one edge.

"Wilbur, we're gonna get it now. Dad's really gonna be mad."

"Don't worry, Clyde. I'll think of something."

Shortly after noon, the movers rolled through the village of Kinderhook, Illinois. Three miles in the distance, they could see Hull where they would turn south off Highway 36 for the last part of their journey toward the river and their new farm.

Leaving Hull, they turned onto a gravel road that took them four miles further to a dirt lane which wound around a slough. At the end of the quarter-mile-long lane stood their new home.

Clyde and Wilbur were anxious to get out and explore. Looking around, they could see the river levee, a short distance west of the house. They headed in that direction.

"Boys," Dad called to them. "We have work to do. You can explore later."

Then the boys remembered the mattress. "We'll unload our truck, Dad," they offered. "And we'll go ahead and set up the beds, too."

Opal was in charge of making all the beds. Carrying an armful of sheets, she walked into the room that she would share with Ruby just as the boys were unfolding the cotton mattress. As they tossed it onto the bed springs, Opal saw the burned spot. "What on earth happened to our mattress? How did it get burned like that?"

"Just don't tell Dad, Opal. Just don't tell Dad. We're busy right now. We'll tell you about it later." The boys rushed out of the room and called to Dad as they ran down the stairs. "The beds are all done. What do you want us to do next?"

"You can get some wood for a fire. Todd and I have finished setting up the cookstove." Glad for a chance to explore the premises, the boys ran outside.

Mom called to Opal and Ruby. "When you girls finish what you're doing, you can start thinking about supper."

The boys brought in an armload of wood and a basket of eggs. "Look at all these eggs," Clyde exclaimed. "The hens laid them in the crates on the way down. Not too many of 'em got broke either."

"That's what we'll have for supper, Opal," Ruby said, taking the eggs from Clyde. "We'll have scrambled eggs and the rest of that apple butter and bread that Mom packed."

A tasty supper and a good night's sleep found the entire family up early and eager to start to work in their new home. And work it would be. Weeds as tall as the kids covered the yard and the pastures. The house needed paint. The barn had a sagging roof.

A herd of brown Swiss cattle, which Dad had bought from the previous owner, roamed the farm at will. Fences were either nonexistent or in total disrepair. Dad helped Clyde and Wilbur hitch a team of horses to a two-section harrow and told them to drag down the weeds so that enough fence rows could be found to enclose the cattle. They found the fence rows the hard way. As if sensing the danger, the team stopped short of strings and coils of barbed wire which had pulled free from rotted fence posts. "Clyde, I can't back up the horses with the harrow behind me. Run and get Dad to help us," Wilbur called as he surveyed his predicament.

"All right." Clyde was more than glad to get a break from the tedious job. "I'll be right back."

But he didn't come right back. After waiting for almost an hour, Wilbur unhooked the team and moved the harrow by hand. The weeds were tall and unyielding — some of the horseweeds stood eight feet tall — but Wilbur freed his team from the dangers of the barbed wire and finished the job Dad had given him.

That evening at the supper table, he asked Clyde, "Where in the world were you? I had to do all the rest of that work by myself."

"Dad needed me," Clyde mumbled, making sure Dad didn't hear him.

Weeks later, Wilbur discovered that Clyde had ridden the tractor with Dad for the remainder of that afternoon.

So began life in the Mississippi River bottoms. For the most part, Dad and Mom traded in Barry and Quincy, Illinois. To avoid paying the toll fee of fifty cents to cross the Mark Twain

Memorial Bridge into Hannibal, Dad usually drove the fifteen miles to Barry. A trip to Quincy was enjoyed only on special occasions or in case of emergencies. Twenty-five miles of gravel road stretched between our home and Quincy, thus making Barry the trading center of choice.

As soon as he helped Dad and Mom get moved into the house, Todd drove back up to the Mason County farm to harvest the fall crops. Pearl and Virginia took time off to help him.

By late fall, all loose ends were gathered. Todd drove the Model T that Dad had bought for five dollars back to Pike County for the last time. About half-way home, the old car blew an oil cap, but he limped it the rest of the way in on three cylinders. A few weeks later Dad sold it for 15 dollars. Dad had a motto: Never buy something that you can't make a dollar on.

Pearl and Virginia returned to work in Peoria where they spent their first Christmas ever away from home. Few gifts were exchanged that Christmas of 1935. The little ones got an orange and candy and small gifts from their sisters in Peoria. Nonetheless, Dad's traditional Christmas gelatine dessert found its way to the holiday dinner table.

This was no ordinary offering. To make his legendary "jello," Dad first went to the cellar and gleaned from its shelves various jars of Mom's home-canned fruit. Next, he and the younger kids cracked and picked out succulent nutmeats from the pecans they had gathered earlier in the fall. Then he peeled and sliced six or eight Christmas oranges and an equal number of bananas. After mixing the jello liquid in a dishpan, Dad dumped in the array of fruit and nuts and a package or two of marshmallows.

"Hm-m-m," he contemplated, as he tasted the marvelous concoction, "I think it needs something else." With that he added at least two pounds of Christmas candy. It was an amazing dessert. And it signaled that the family was settling into their new Pike County home.

Chapter 4

My Sunshine Sister

Emotions are among the toughest things in the world to manufacture out of whole cloth; it is easier to manufacture seven facts than one emotion.

"Life on the Mississippi"

Mom always called Opal the sunshine of our household. She wasn't a "goody-two-shoes" kind of sister; she was one of those wonderful, gentle young girls that everyone loved.

From the beginning, Opal was pleasant. "Opal was an easy baby to handle," Mom would say. "She almost never fussed or cried. When she did, her tears fell like big pearl drops down her rosy cheeks. I always knew there was something wrong when Opal cried."

Once, when Opal was about fifteen months old, Aunt Sarah came to help Mom do some wallpapering. Dad and Mom had just moved to the place, and the house was in need of some cleaning up.

Knowing she couldn't entice Todd to stay indoors and watch his baby sister, Mom placed the responsibility for Opal's whereabouts in the hands of five-year-old Pearl. Since the bedroom that was being papered adjoined the living room where the children would be playing, Mom was within hearing distance, so she felt comfortable leaving Opal in Pearl's care. However, she didn't consider Todd's influence and well she should have, because Todd and Pearl were inseparable.

"Pearl, c'mere. Look what I found." Todd was standing on the kitchen step calling to her through the screen door. Leaving her small charge in the middle of the living room floor, Pearl ran out into the kitchen. Todd was holding the biggest bull frog she had ever seen. "C'mon out and see him jump," Todd invited. The little babysitter accepted her big brother's invitation and joined him out in the yard. Opal toddled out to the kitchen.

A serving bowl of stewed prunes left to cool for the noon meal caught the baby girl's attention. Chubby hands procured two of the juicy morsels and, as is the custom of all babies, the prunes went from hands to mouth.

In the meantime, Pearl and Todd lost interest in the jumping bullfrog and began to heed the growls of their stomachs — time to go in for dinner. When they stepped into the kitchen, they saw Opal standing beside the cupboard shelf which held the prune bowl. She was contentedly clapping her sticky hands together. The bowl was almost empty. It held only a few smashed prunes and some seeds.

"Mom, I think Opal ate some prunes," Pearl said to Mom who was just coming into the room to fix a bite to eat.

"Oh, Pearl, did you let her have all those prunes? Did you and Todd or Virginia or Ruby eat any?"

"No," came the small reply.

Mom called the doctor who said to watch the baby closely for the next couple of days and so they did. Nothing happened. Opal didn't get sick. She didn't pass any seeds. Considering the number of the seeds left in the bowl, Mom had already assumed (and hoped) that none had been swallowed by the family prune eater.

Fourteen years later, Opal would again innocently imbibe in some "forbidden fruit." And the occasion would happen because of yet another move — the move to Pike County.

Fifteen-year-old Opal and sixteen-year-old Ruby enjoyed

their new home. They helped Mom with the younger kids and the housework while Todd, Wilbur, and Clyde were Dad's farm hands. To earn money, the two girls picked up pecans and sold them for a nickel a pound. Pecan trees were abundant on the new farm.

At first, Mom, too, enjoyed her new home, but during that first winter, she began to tire easily. Early one spring morning of 1936 while Opal and Ruby were packing school lunches, Mom came into the kitchen with quite an unexpected announcement, "Girls, we're going to get another baby."

"Oh, Mom," they cried. "When? Is that why you haven't been feeling so good lately?"

"Yes, that's why I haven't been feeling very good. The worse part about it is that I keep having such awful headaches. I'm going to have to depend on the both of you to help me take care of the house and do the cooking. We'll make it; don't worry. I'll go ahead and make up the beds this morning. You two can clean up the breakfast dishes when you're through with the lunches." Mom smiled, but the girls could see that she wasn't feeling well.

Babies weren't new in the Dunker household, but being four hours away from friends and family was new. "Well, I guess it's up to us, Opal," Ruby stated when Mom left the kitchen. "Pearl and Virginia won't be able to come home to help us either."

"Ruby, I'm worried about Mom. She hasn't looked a bit good. Do you think this will be too much for her?"

"There's nothing we can do about it now, Opal. Let's finish these lunches and as soon as we get the kitchen cleaned up, we'll go do the washing."

The wash house stood about fifty feet across the yard to the north of the kitchen. It was a drafty old building with no stove inside it. "I'll fill the reservoir and the copper boiler. That way the water should be hot by the time we get the breakfast dishes done." Opal filled the water reservoir which was attached to the end of the cookstove. Then she got the copper boiler out. "I'll have Clyde and Wilbur fill this before they go to school 'cause they can carry it easier than I can."

As soon as the wash water was heated, Dad helped the girls carry it to the wash house. Then he started the noisy gasoline engine which powered the washing machine. "Looks like you girls are going to have a cold wash day," he observed, emptying the last bucket of steaming water into the rinse tub. "It even feels like snow. If you need anything, I'll be workin' in the barn this morning."

"I think Dad's right, Opal. Look how gray the sky is. It looks like we're gonna get some snow. Let's hurry." The agitator monotonously churned homemade lye soap into the dirty clothes while the girls took turns forcing individual pieces through the ringer and into the rinse tub. A cold northeast wind blew up and whistled through the cracks in the board floor, teasing about their ankles and legs.

"Boy, I'm cold, Ruby," Opal said, dancing first on one foot and then the other. With cupped hands she caught her warm breath to thaw freezing fingers. "Ruby, as soon as you get that tubful run through, let's go get some more hot water and warm up for a minute in the kitchen."

"While we're in there, remind me to get another bar of soap. I sure wish we had something else to use besides this soap Mom makes. It's hard to rinse out of the clothes."

"Yes, but it sure gets the clothes clean. All we need to do is keep plenty of hot water on hand to rinse with. Good, you've finished that tubful. I'll hang them out when we get back. Let's go on in before we freeze, Ruby."

But the day had turned so cold that each new addition of hot water wouldn't keep the rinse water hot for any length of time. The girls found themselves making frequent trips to the house for hot water. On one of the trips into the house, Ruby turned to Opal. "Say, you know that medicinal whiskey that Dad keeps in the cupboard? Why don't we each take a sip of it? It'll warm us up."

"Ruby, do you think we should? It is whiskey, you know."

"Yes, but it's medicinal whiskey. Dad gives it to the livestock when they're sick or cold. I'm gonna take a sip. You can if you want to."

"It is cold out there. Oh, all right. Just one sip." Opal took a taste from the bottle of "medicinal whiskey." "Whew, it does taste awful, doesn't it?"

"Yes, but I think I'm warmer already. Grab that bucket of hot water, Opal, and let's go. We'll be through in no time."

After making two or three more trips each into the house, each time sipping from the wonderful warming elixir, the girls were able to finish the washing in record time. Slipping and sliding across the soapy-water covered wash house floor, they giggled their way through the last of the dirty clothes.

"There, the throw rugs are hanging on the fence and we're done," Opal announced as she stepped back into the wash house. "Now, I'll help you empty this water and we can go in."

Flurries of snow melted against their flushed faces as they carried buckets of water from the rinse tubs and emptied them over the fence. "I sure have warmed up, Opal. I can see why Dad gives that whiskey to his animals."

"I'm warmer, too," Opal agreed, "and I don't know when we've got the washing done so fast. But maybe the weather is getting warmer."

Ruby began to giggle. "Warmer? How can that be? It's snowing." Both girls dissolved in a fit of giggles.

"We've gotta settle down and go get dinner on," Ruby reminded Opal. They turned the emptied rinse tubs upside down and started toward the kitchen porch.

Ruby was first to stumble onto the porch. As she reached for the kitchen door, Todd opened it and came out onto the porch. "I cleaned the rabbits I got this morning. Where's Mom? Can you girls fix the rabbits for dinner? I put them in the kitchen sink. Come in here and I'll show you."

Dutifully, the two rosy-cheeked, smiling girls followed their older brother into the kitchen. But instead of directing them to the rabbits in the sink, Todd stood at the kitchen table. "What's this doing out?" he asked, holding up the whiskey bottle. "Have you girls been drinking this stuff? Don't you know it's for the livestock?"

Opal was still standing at the kitchen door. She smiled at

him, her bright, blue eyes sparkling a little more than usual. Tripping over the throw-rug at the kitchen door, she stumbled over to the table and examined the bottle closely. "We just took a teeny little sip to keep us warm, Todd. I don't think we drank very much. There's quite a bit left in here. Isn't that what it's for, to warm people?"

Ruby laughed. "We didn't do anything wrong and we got the washing done, didn't we?"

The warm kitchen had deteriorated Opal's condition even further. With one shoulder slightly drooping and a silly grin on her face, she placed her hands squarely on her hips and came to Ruby's defense. "Ruby's absholutely right, Todd."

Ruby smiled in surprised agreement. She was unaccustomed to the defensive action of the usually soft spoken Opal. Todd, too, was astonished.

"Well, I guess you're right. Not too much of this stuff is gone, but you two had better never drink any of it again. Those rabbits are in the sink. I brought in some fresh water so you could rinse them before you fry them. I'll go check on Mom."

As soon as Todd left the kitchen, a rather pale Opal turned to Ruby. "I feel sick."

"Don't get sick on me now. We have to get dinner. Here's some coffee left from breakfast. Drink it. It should make you feel better."

"I wish I'd used coffee instead of whiskey to warm up with this morning," complained Opal as she gulped down the steaming beverage. "I think I'll listen to Todd after this."

Mom, who had been resting in her room that morning, came into the kitchen as the girls were putting the meal on the table. "Are you all right, Opal. You look a little peaked."

"I'm fine, Mom. Are Dad and the boys ready for dinner? Where's June and Garnette?" Opal hurried about the kitchen doing everything she could to divert Mom's attention.

After filling coffee cups and milk glasses and seating the small children, the two girls sat down at the table. Quietly they picked at their food.

"You two are awful quiet. Something wrong?" Dad asked.

But he didn't wait for their answer because he was concerned about some livestock. "Todd, we should throw down some extra hay. This cold snap may last a little while."

When the meal was over and the dishes were done, the two tired and somewhat nauseous girls brought the washing into the house. Most of it was frozen and had to be propped and draped over the kitchen table and chairs and over chairs in the living room.

As they crawled into bed that night, they could hear Dad banking the stove in the living room.

"Ruby, do you think Todd told Dad?" Opal asked.

"If he did, he did, Opal. Goodnight."

The girls heard Dad walking toward the stairway.

"Oh, no, he's probably gonna come up and bawl us out," Opal whispered.

But instead, only Dad's familiar bedtime words drifted up the stairs. "Goodnight, girls; goodnight boys." And the house was quiet.

Throughout her life, Opal's sunshine personality remained constant. She left us in the spring of 1987, but I know that Heaven is just a little brighter because of her presence.

Chapter 5

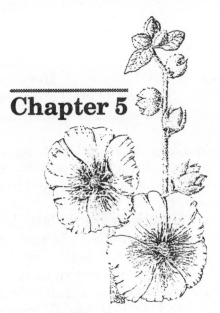

Surviving

*I am hurt all over, but I cannot tell the full extent
yet, because the doctor is not done taking inventory.*

"Sketches New and Old"

Cold weather was over and mid-May offered promise.
Mom's morning sickness had finally subsided, but her
headaches still hung on.

Early one May morning, she met Dad at the breakfast table
with news. "Charlie," she began, "Wilbur and Clyde aren't
going to be able to help you with the chores this morning.
They're both sick. Garnette and Dickie are complaining, too."

"What's the matter?"

"I guess they have the spring flu. They're all complaining
of stomach aches. Clyde and Wilbur have been sick most of
the night. I hope the little kids don't get it."

"How are you feeling, Corrie? If you need anything, Todd
and I will be in the barn." Dad pushed his chair from the
breakfast table. "Come on, Todd, we'd better get started.
We're not going to have any help this morning."

"I'm all right," Mom told Dad. "Ruby and Opal are good to
help."

But Mom wasn't "all right." Her headache had started before she got up. And the little ones did get the flu. By late afternoon everyone was either vomiting or running to the toilet or both.

Dad, Todd, Ruby, and Opal escaped the ailment and kept things going until everyone got well. Everyone, that is, except Wilbur. He was so sick that he couldn't even go out to the pasture to see the new colt.

For the rest of the kids, the flu lasted about 24 to 36 hours, but Wilbur kept complaining of stomach pain.

"Charlie, I think you'd better take him up to see Dr. Ailshire. Something's just not right here."

"All right, Clyde can ride along with us. We shouldn't be too long." Dad and Clyde helped Wilbur into the Model A and drove the fifteen-mile trip to Plainville to the doctor's office.

A quick examination of Wilbur caused a look of concern to flash across Dr. Ailshire's face. "I'll tell you what, Charlie. Why don't you and the boys get in my car and we'll drive up to Quincy to the hospital. I'd like a colleague of mine to take a look at your boy."

"I've got my car, Doc. I can..."

"Don't worry. I'll bring you back as soon as we get the boy where he needs to be. Then you can pick up your car."

Dad conceded and helped Wilbur into the doctor's long, black car and a speedy trip was made to Quincy with Dr. Ailshire's driver at the wheel. Clyde and Dad sat in the back seat with Wilbur. The boys had never seen such a fancy car and would have enjoyed the ride had it not been for the obvious seriousness of the situation.

Dr. Caddick was waiting for them at the hospital. Clyde stood close to Dad as nurses rushed Wilbur into an examining room. The doctor completed the examination quickly, then he turned and looked at Dad.

"We're going to have to perform emergency surgery, Mr. Dunker." Dr. Caddick's face was grave. "Your son has a ruptured appendix. Blood tests have confirmed Dr. Ailshire's suspicions."

"Can we see him before his surgery?"

"Sure. The nurse will show you where he is."

Dad and Clyde followed the nurse to a room where they found a very groggy Wilbur waiting to be wheeled into surgery.

"Don't you worry, now, Wilbur," Dad tried to comfort him. "You're gonna be just fine."

Wilbur smiled. "I'll be all right, Dad," he mumbled in agreement and drifted off into a drugged sleep.

"Dad," Clyde pulled at his father's sleeve, "we'd better take Wilbur's clothes home. He might never need 'em again."

Dad's heart leaped in his throat. Clyde's innocent statement was all too real.

"I can take you back to get your car, now, Charlie, if you'd like, or would you rather wait until surgery is over?" Dr. Ailshire placed a comforting hand on Dad's shoulder. "It'll take at least two hours."

"Let's go, then. I can get on down home and let the wife know what's going on and get back up here. Will I have that much time before he wakes up?"

"Sure, Charlie, sure."

Dad and Clyde climbed into Dr. Ailshire's car. They made the trip from Quincy to Plainville in silence. When they reached Dad's car, he turned to Dr. Ailshire, "What's his chances, Doc?"

"Maybe fifty/fifty. We'll see, Charlie, we'll see."

A troubled silence filled the little Model A car as Dad and Clyde hurried home to give the bad news to the rest of the family.

"Todd, you go into Hull and call Pearl and Virginia. Then come on back home and stay with your mother and the rest of the kids. (Pearl and Virginia were still working as maids in Peoria.) Tell the girls that Wilbur is pretty bad, and he might not make it. Doc says he has a fifty/fifty chance. Tell them to try to come home if they can. I'm going on back to the hospital. Opal, you and Ruby keep an eye on your mom. Her headache is awful. She can't come up to the hospital right now, not the way she feels. If she doesn't quit throwing up, you might have to take her up to see Doc Ailshire. I'll come home as soon as I can and let you know how things are."

Ruby followed Dad outside. "Dad, didn't you say that Wilbur has a fifty/fifty chance? Well, that means he has a fifty percent chance of making it, too."

"Sure, Ruby, sure." Dad climbed into the car and drove back to Quincy. He waited alone at the hospital.

"Mr. Dunker?" Pulling off his mask, Dr. Caddick sat down next to Dad. "Surgery's over and I'll tell you just what we did. We opened your boy up, laid his intestines out on the table, washed them and sprinkled them with a new drug called Sulfa. Then we sprinkled the open area with Sulfa and put everything back in place and closed the incision. Now, what all of us can do is wait and pray."

Back at home, Mom couldn't stand the wait any longer. Her headache had let up enough to allow her to get out of bed, so she put on a clean dress and combed her hair "Todd, take me up to see Wilbur," she demanded. If you won't drive me up to that hospital, I'll do it myself. I still know how to drive."

"But Mom, Dad said he would let us know. Why don't you just stay here and try to get over your headache? If we don't hear shortly, I'll take you up."

"My headache won't be any worse up there than it is waiting here, Todd. Please take me," Mom pleaded, tears streaming down her cheeks.

"All right, all right. I'll take you."

Even though he was worried about her and knew she felt miserable, Dad was relieved to see Mom come into the waiting room. "The doctor was just here, Corrie. He said everything went all right, but Wilbur's a sick boy."

"Where is he? I want to see him." Mom would know just how sick Wilbur was when she could see him for herself.

The nurse came into the waiting room. "Mr. and Mrs. Dunker? Your son is in his room now, but he still very groggy. You may go in, but don't tire him."

Mom stood by Wilbur's bed for a long time, holding his hand. Finally the nurse put her arm around my weary mother's shoulders. "Mrs. Dunker, he's resting. Why don't you let Mr. Dunker take you home for a little while? We'll take care of Wilbur."

The first week of Wilbur's post-operative care was touch and go. Virginia gave up her job in Peoria and came home to help out. The doctor made arrangements for an extra bed to be placed in the hospital room, and Virginia moved in with her convalescing brother.

When Mom's health allowed, Dad took her to the hospital for visits. The long vigil lasted about two weeks. Finally Dr. Caddick could offer Mom and Dad hope for a full recovery.

"He's been a real trouper. We're going to miss him," Dr. Caddick smiled on the day of Wilbur's release. "I don't know what you folks feed those youngsters, but I can tell you this — if it wasn't for his excellent general health, things might not have gone so well."

The day finally came when Wilbur was released from the hospital. The cot in the living room had been made into a bed for the recuperating boy so that he could be close to Mom and Dad's downstairs bedroom. Clyde was the first to greet him when the car pulled into the lot.

"Come on out to the pasture and see the colt that was born the day you got sick," he invited, as Dad and Mom helped Wilbur from the car.

"He can't go out there just yet, Clyde," Mom laughed. "He has to stay in bed for awhile."

Not wanting his brother to have to wait another minute before seeing the new offspring, Clyde did the next best thing. He roped the young colt and led him to the living room window by Wilbur's cot. And so the wobbly legged colt met his pale, wobbly-legged counterpart nose to nose through the window screen.

I suppose Wilbur's ruptured appendix was the most frightening illness in the lives of the Dunker kids, except for the close call Virginia had when she was about twelve.

The year was 1929. During the winter Virginia and the rest of the kids caught colds. Everyone developed a cough, but Mom's home remedies took care of the ailing brood, and it looked as though health was restored to all. However, Virginia's cough was different. Even after the rest of the kids were well and no longer coughing, her ailment lingered, and her general health began to deteriorate.

Heeding the advice of their family doctor, Dad and Mom drove her into Peoria to see a pediatrician who immediately ordered chest x-rays.

"Mr. and Mrs. Dunker?" The nurse called them into the doctor's office. A serious and concerned expression met them across the desk. "I'm afraid I have bad news. Your daughter has tuberculosis."

My stunned and frightened parents caught random words and phrases — "bed rest," "plenty of fresh fruits and vegetables," "invalid," as the doctor gave them instructions and suggestions for Virginia's care.

Winter wore into spring as the whole family pitched in to make their patient as comfortable as possible. Pearl, Virginia's head nurse, made all of her favorite foods and waited on her every need.

The attention worked. The shut-in improved. When the weather warmed, Mom allowed her to go outside. One day, Dad let her ride into town with him. As a special treat, he bought her an ice cream cone. Then on the way home, the cough returned. Dad feared that Virginia was suffering a setback. When they got home, he lifted the coughing child from the car. Virginia leaned against the fence and coughed until she finally vomited.

That day marked the beginning of the end of the disease. A day or two later, Mom and Dad took her back to Peoria to keep an appointment for a checkup.

"Mr. and Mrs. Dunker," the doctor came into the waiting room to greet them with a most bizarre message. "I have some good news for you. Your daughter's x-rays were mixed up with another patient. Virginia does not have tuberculosis. From the x-rays she appears to have suffered from a severe chest congestion. How is she?"

"She's fine; she's just fine." Mom was stunned. "She had a bad coughing spell a couple of days ago. When she got over that she seemed to start getting better overnight."

"The cough probably loosened the congestion and brought

it up. I'll examine her, but I'm sure she's on her way to recovery." The doctor smiled and stepped into the examining room.

Mom's emotions ran the gamut. She laughed; she cried, and then she became angry. To think that they had suffered all that mental anguish due to a mis-diagnosis. But Virginia's health had improved and finally returned to normal and that was the important issue.

Other than Todd's broken shoulder due to a fall from the family pony, Virginia's almost-tuberculosis in 1929 and Wilbur's ruptured appendix in 1936 were the most extraordinary and traumatic illnesses to occur in our family. Unless you would consider my birth extraordinary and traumatic. And you could.

Two months after experiencing the stress of Wilbur's illness and recovery, Mom's difficult pregnancy came to an end. I decided to make my arrival.

A record heat wave was scorching the Midwest on July 9, 1936, but I paid it no heed. During the late afternoon of that day, with the temperature soaring above the 100-degree mark, Mom sent Dad for Dr. Ailshire. Todd hurried over to our neighbors, the Robbins family, and brought their mother to be with Mom until Dad and the doctor could get back.

"Charlie, you're a lucky man to have 12 such healthy children. What are you looking for this time?" Doctor Ailshire asked as he scrubbed in our kitchen sink.

"A healthy baby, Doc. But I was telling a friend the other day that it'd be nice if we would get twins; that way we'd skip that unlucky number, 13."

Dr. Ailshire laughed. "I don't think you're going to get your wish, but we'll see what we can do. Hand me that towel."

At ten o'clock that evening I was born, all ten pounds and twelve ounces of me. Doctor Ailshire held me up for Mom to see. "Look there, Mrs. Dunker. She's a fine one with eyes as black as coal. You get some rest now. You've done a fine job. We'll take care of this little lady for awhile."

Mrs. Robbins bathed and dressed me and gently placed me in the only baby bed Mom had. Not anticipating the arrival

of a 13th child, Dad and Mom didn't move the baby bed to
Pike County, so Mom arranged two dining chairs, front edges
together, between her bed and the wall to create my first bed.
A feather pillow became my first mattress and a pillow case
my sheet.

Mom and Dad's family now numbered twelve, plus me.

My birth would seem to have been almost anti-climatic
considering the seriousness of Wilbur's illness and his
miraculous recovery, but it wasn't. Years later, Mom and Dad
would tell the story of my birth with the same love and
concern that they felt when telling anything about any of
their children. But they always prefaced the story with a
description of the oppressive heat of that year.

The heat wave sent thermometers soaring to record
heights. Dad and the boys slept outside in the yard. The girls
slept on the south kitchen porch.

Mom suffered a breast infection which resulted in her
inability to nurse her 13th child. When I was three days old,
she sent Dad to town for baby bottles. Twice daily she made
formula from cow's milk and Karo Syrup. She poured it into
sterilized quart jars and dropped it from a rope down into the
well to keep it cool.

Diminutive black bugs, which Mom called oat bugs, came
through the screens of her bedroom windows. They bit both
of us. She hung wet dish towels over the screens to block the
miniscule intruders and to try to cool the room.

Some of Dad's hogs succumbed to the heat. He dragged
their bloated carcasses quite a distance south of the house
and burned them. Just about the only breeze that stirred
during those hot July days, came that day, causing the putrid
smoke from the burning hog carcasses to find its way toward
the house and into Mom's bedroom.

The only crop that made any money at all was the spring
wheat. The corn and soybeans burned up. But Dad's in-
genuity and Mom's strength saw us through.

Pearl came home from Peoria that summer to get acquainted with her baby sister and to announce that she would
be getting married in December. With her welcomed return

home, 13 Dunker children, ranging in ages from 21 to infant, filled every corner of our Pike County home. Even though it was only for a few months, Mom and Dad had their entire brood under one roof.

As if in celebration of Mom and Dad's first year in Pike County, President Franklin D. Roosevelt made a visit to the area. That fall, the President's long motorcade snaked along U. S. Route 36. The President dedicated the newly built Mark Twain Memorial Bridge which linked west-central Illinois to Hannibal, Missouri.

Other than being encouraged to vote when we came of age, Mom and Dad rarely discussed politics with us kids. However, I do know that they had no trouble deciding where to cast their vote when Roosevelt ran for office. Mom had read somewhere that Roosevelt was an advocate of big families for America's farms. I am almost certain that this alleged advocacy was the reason he got Mom's vote and probably swayed Dad's vote, too.

The entire family walked, rode in the truck, or rode horses up to Highway 36 to get a glimpse of their president and to wave at him. They had survived their first year in Pike County; Wilbur had survived a ruptured appendix; Mom and I survived the record heat wave of 1936.

It all goes to prove that families can survive the toughest times when they stick together.

Chapter 6

Sparrows in the Wedding Bed

...A good and wholesome thing is a little harmless fun in this world; it tones a body up and keeps him human and prevents him from souring.

Mark Twain

Poor Pauline. She and Todd spent their wedding night at our house. Its not that she didn't know us; before their marriage she had spent the summer, fall, and early winter of 1937 with us. But that didn't mean she wanted to spend her wedding night with us. And she certainly didn't want sparrows in her wedding bed.

Todd had asked this dark-haired young girl with the bubbly laugh and sparkling brown eyes to come from Glasford, Illinois and stay with us in Pike county because he couldn't take the time off to make the four-hour trip to visit her as often as he wanted. And he wanted her here because he planned for them to be married sometime during the summer. "As soon as we get some bad weather so that I can't work," Todd promised, "we'll get married." He worked for the U. S. Army Corp of Engineers and helped Dad when he could. Jobs were so hard to get that he didn't want to jeopardize this one by asking for time off just to get married.

In the meantime, on August 6, pretty Opal — Mom's sunshine girl — married Lawrence "Dode" Kroencke. During their courting days, Dode would sometimes leave his car on the gravel road and walk down the lane to our house. Even though Dad's mean bull (Mom's "gentleman cow") chased him down that lane a few times, Dode perservered. He and Opal set up housekeeping on a farm about ten miles north of us. Todd and Pauline still waited. The coveted bad weather would not materialize.

After a seemingly endless wait, true love and bad weather finally came together. On December 14, 1937, Charles Franklin Dunker, firstborn of my Mom and Dad, married Pauline Arnold.

Dode and Opal had invited the newlyweds to spend their wedding night in the recently established Kroencke household, but the wonderful bad weather which had made the wedding possible, interfered with the honeymoon. Icy roads forced the young couple to stay at our house.

Mom readied the spare bedroom and my brother and his bride were welcomed. Before they retired for the night, Mom fixed them a light wedding supper which she and Dad enjoyed with them

While the four adults were eating, Wilbur and Clyde sneaked out to the barn and caught ten or twelve sparrows each. With birds stuffed in their pockets and down inside their coats, the two miscreants strolled nonchalantly across the kitchen floor bidding all a friendly goodnight. Then they scurried up the stairs. The boys hid most of the sparrows in the slop jar, slipping the remainder between the sheets of the wedding bed.

The next morning at the breakfast table, three-year-old June asked, "Pauline, why didn't you sleep with me last night? How come you slept with Todd? You always sleep with me and Garnette."

Pauline blushed crimson and Mom changed the subject. Clyde and Wilbur waited in vain for Todd to say something about the sparrows, but no acknowledgment was forthcoming, and the disappointed boys went off to school.

That evening after supper, Mom said plenty about the sparrows in the guest bed and about the bird feathers all over the room. The two pranksters were left with the full realization that Mom didn't appreciate the wedding night joke. But they thought it was funny.

Pearl had married Karl Maple in December of 1936. They rented an apartment in Peoria. On September 23, 1937, Nancy Jo Maple was born. Mom and Dad became "Grandma and Grandpa Dunker" and I became "Aunt Pat." I was fifteen months old. Virginia married Herbert "Duff" Schulz in October of 1938. They rented a farm near Mason City. In 1939 Ruby moved to Peoria, leaving only eight Dunker children at home.

Wilbur and Clyde were Dad's farm hands and Garnette and Mom kept the house going. The three little boys, as Dick, Johnnie, and Billie were called, and June and I brought up the rear.

Farm prices gradually improved. Dad and the boys painted the house and repaired the screened-in kitchen porches. Mom papered and painted inside the house and a pump was installed in the kitchen. The roof on the old barn was repaired and raised, creating a gambrel roof. Dad asked our landlord, Mr. Heckman, for a badly needed second barn and the request was granted. It began to appear that Dad's decision to move to Pike County had been a wise one. In 1939, he was able to buy a new pickup truck.

Twice yearly Mr. Heckman and Mrs. Heckman (we never, ever called them by their first names) visited their Pike County property. They usually stayed in a little house at the end of our lane which we nicknamed "the cottage." We looked forward to their coming with the same delicious anticipation that we felt while waiting in the kitchen closet under the stairs for the arrival of Santa Claus.

When someone yelled, "The Heckmans' car is coming down the lane!" we kids lined up along the front yard fence. Dick, Johnnie, Billie, June, Garnette and I stood in eager anticipation. Garnette held my hand tightly as the Heckmans' new

Buick purred down our dirt lane, rolling to a stop in the lot
near the hollyhock- and child-lined fence.

Mr. and Mrs. Heckman brought candy — not a taste-bud-
teasing teeny sack of candy, but a grocery-size brown paper
bag filled with smaller sacks of licorice, jelly beans, orange
slices, candy corn, and hard candy of every description.

Mr. Heckman got out of the car first and walked around to
open the door for his stylish wife. We saw her white shoe-clad
foot step onto our dusty lot, followed by the hem of her
summer voile dress as she emerged into full view. She quickly
flashed a broad smile which set everybody at ease. Mrs.
Heckman always seemed genuinely glad to see us.

She and Mr. Heckman shook hands with Mom and Dad,
then she brushed a stray wisp of white hair from her face and
asked in a casual tone, "Louis, did you put anything in the
back of the car for Mr. and Mrs. Dunker's children?"

The tall, dignified man, outfitted in a gray summer suit,
took on a serious look and replied, "Well, let's see, now. I hope
I remembered to put that bag back here." Then he opened the
back door of the car and produced the candy.

Finally, the bag started along the line of Dunkers. When it
came to me, I knew to take only one piece. But I didn't mind,
because I knew that the rest of the candy would stay after
the Heckmans left.

The Heckmans didn't go home empty handed either. Mom
and Dad always gave them a tour of the truck patch and our
kitchen garden, filling a bushel basket with farm bounty.
During one of their visits, Mrs. Heckman particularly enjoyed the four o'clocks that Dad had planted near the end of
the hollyhocks.

Before he could stop her, Dad saw Mrs. Heckman picking
up small, round, black "seeds" from beneath the fuchsia
colored flowers. "Bring me a container from the car, Louis,"
she called to her husband, "I'm going to take a bunch of these
seeds so that I can have some of these beautiful flowers in
our yard."

Mom nudged Dad who only smiled. When the Heckmans
left that day, Dad said to Clyde and Wilbur, "You boys had

better pen those little goats. They've been nibbling on my four
o'clocks again."

"Charlie, why didn't you tell her?" Mom laughed.

"I don't know; I just didn't," Dad chuckled. "What do you
think, Corrie? Do you suppose Mrs. Heckman's four o'clocks
will bloom next summer?"

We loved their visits. We never felt less than the Heckmans; they were simply another dimension of our lives. Mr.
Heckman and Dad were business partners and respected
each other as such. And Mom seemed to be just as comfortable seating them at our meal table as she did any other
visitor in our home. They may have been the landlord and
the landlady, but we knew them only as Mr. and Mrs.
Heckman, the people with whom Dad farmed.

Other than the Heckmans, we received few "outsiders" as
visitors. It didn't matter. We made our own fun.

During winter months we played fox and goose on the
snow-covered pond south of the house. For a special sweet
treat, Mom added cream ("top milk" is what she called it),
vanilla, and sugar to a dishpan filled with new fallen snow,
and we had snow ice cream.

Spring jaunts into the pasture with Dad to check for new-
born lambs was a special time. When an unexpected cold spell
blew in during lambing time, Dad brought the tiny wooly
babies into the kitchen. With gentle hands he rubbed frisky
life into the wobbly legged creatures, leaving them behind
the cookstove until he could coax the ewe into the shed.

A special summer treat was ice cream made in the hand-
cranked freezer. However, I'll never forget my first real ice
cream cone. One momentous day, June and I begged a ride
to Hull with Dad.

"How would you two like an ice cream cone before we go
home?" Dad offered, climbing back into the truck after the
completion of his errands. "We'll get one right here at
Buchanan's."

Dad stopped in front of the little restaurant and hurried
inside. We waited in the truck. A lifetime later he returned,
carrying the two double-dip treats. "You'll have to eat fast

'cause it's hot, and the ice cream will melt and make a mess."
This ice cream was different from Mom's ice cream. I didn't
see the need to hurry, because it wasn't melting as fast as
homemade ice cream. But Dad was right. The point of my
cone soon became slightly soggy. A tiny drop of warm ice
cream dropped on my leg.

"Don't eat the point off," Dad warned. He had seen me tip
my cone to survey my predicament. It would seem that what
I did next was in direct defiance of Dad's order, but it wasn't.
I really thought it would correct a messy situation. I bit the
point off. Unfortunately, my plan to suck the melted ice
cream from the narrow, now opened end of the cone was not
thoroughly considered. When I tipped the cone, the top dip
fell into my lap. And when I righted the cone to replace the
top dip, the sweet mixture, no longer iced, ran from the
open-ended cone down my arm and dripped from my elbow
onto the truck seat.

Dad laughed. "You'll know better next time," was all he
said.

Summer fun also included firefly chases after the sun
dipped behind the river bluff on the Missouri side. Many a
summer night's catch of lightening bugs, as we called them,
expired in the confines of Mom's fruit jars as the mysterious
little insects winked us to sleep from dresser tops.

Bill was the best lightening bug catcher. One night when
he and I and June were chasing the elusive little creatures,
Bill observed that we could catch more if we ran through the
pasture south of the house. "Don't go out there," Dad warned.
"There's chiggers in that pasture. You'll be eaten alive."

We gave up on the pasture idea, at least June and I did,
and took our existing catch into the house. The next evening
the pasture's offering of lightening bugs again tempted Bill.
He succumbed to the call.

"Mom," he complained the next morning, "my legs itch all
over and they're covered with some kind of bites."

"Billie," Mom asked, "Did you go into that pasture south of
the house? If you did, you're covered with chigger bites."

The daring trip to the south pasture had repercussions far

more serious than plain chigger bites. Boils. Bill's bites became infected and 21 boils developed on his legs — nine on one and 12 on the other. The champion lightening bug catcher became a very sick little boy. Mom kept Bill in bed for about three weeks. June and I appointed ourselves as his nurses. Mom did need help with the extra small chores created by her invalid, but we had a tendency to overdo it. Often, our feverish, eight-year-old brother mustered all the strength he could and yelled, "Mom, get the girls out of here!"

Every day, Mom soaked Bill's swollen legs with hot boric acid poultices and wrapped them with bandages onto which she had smeared Rawleigh's Black Salve. This dependable remedy healed the boils, but it took awhile for Bill to get back on his feet. The massive infection that had invaded his legs left his body weak.

June and I became his crutches. The pale boy balanced himself between the two of us. Amid fits of falling down giggles, patience and impatience, and tears, Bill walked again.

A galvanized foot tub set on the kitchen porch during the summer months. "Did you kids wash your feet before you came in?" was a nightly question. One evening, June, Bill, and I went wading in the muddy part of the slough that ran along the north side of our front yard — out beyond the chicken yard. It had been created by seep water from the Mississippi.

Gooey, thick mud coated our legs from our feet to our knees. We let the mud dry and called the resulting mess "mud stockings." "It'll help keep the mosquitoes and chiggers off our legs," Bill declared. June and I should have realized right then that the mud was going to get us into trouble. After all, who was Bill to tell anyone how to avoid chiggers? Nevertheless, we listened to him.

I probably listened because he was smart enough to catch small garter snakes and curl them around his wrists like bracelets. That feat alone revealed extreme bravery, and bravery to my six-year-old way of thinking, indicated great wisdom. June could do it too. I chose to remain the onlooker.

I don't know who came up with the idea, but we decided to sneak into our beds that night, mud stockings in place. "When Mom and Dad call us in to bed, we'll just splash our hands in the foot tub and make them think we washed our feet," we agreed.

The screen door squeaked, betraying our entry into the kitchen. Mom and Dad called to us from the living room. "Did you kids wash the mud off your feet and legs before you came in?"

"Sure," we answered, feeling only a little trace of guilt, and scurried across the kitchen to the stairway. We slept in our mud stockings that night. I don't know why — it just seemed like a good idea. I don't remember what Mom said when she saw the dried mud in our beds. Knowing how particular Mom was with her beds, I'll bet she said plenty.

A section of that slough which had provided the mud for our stockings boasted of a sand and gravel bottom. It was our swimming hole when we could talk Mom into letting us play there. Dad built a foot bridge across the 20 foot expanse of water. Sometimes he threw the boys off the bridge into the water. They came up kicking and sputtering, but always laughing. It looked like a lot of fun.

I asked Dad to throw me in. I came up kicking and sputtering too, but not laughing. I never asked to be thrown from the foot bridge again.

The chicken house stood between the slough and the north yard. Everybody had a job and my job was egg gathering. I didn't like it. I was always glad that the north kitchen porch was close to the chicken yard gate when a disgruntled rooster got after me.

We had a particularly intimidating rooster who tried to attack anyone he saw entering his domain. I was afraid of him and he knew it. Somehow, though, I managed to escape him until the day I threw a grouchy setting hen from her nest. Her squawk of disapproval upset the rooster. He ran for me as I flung open the chicken yard gate and dashed for the kitchen porch.

Before I could reach the safety of the porch, he spread his wings and leaped on my back. He hung on, squawking and flapping while I screamed, "He-el-l-lp, he-el-l-lp!"

Seeing my predicament, Johnnie grabbed a board and hit the rooster. The feathered monster fell to the ground with a thud. "Oh, oh, I think I killed him," my brave brother moaned. Mom ran out of the house to see what all the commotion was about. "I think I killed the mean rooster, Mom," Johnnie admitted.

Mom understood. "Don't worry about it. Just throw him up on the porch and I'll dress him later." She took the egg bucket from me and directed me into the house. "Now, we'll see if that darned rooster scratched your back." Mom's gentle hands lifted my shirt as she checked for scratches.

The rooster didn't hurt me, but I was glad to see Mom put the kettle on to boil. I knew what the next step would be. A quick dip in the boiling hot water would make feather plucking or "dressing" the rooster much easier for Mom and would make egg gathering much easier for me. When Mom opened the porch door to retrieve the fallen bird, he leaped at her. Johnnie had only stunned the king of the chicken yard. Mom returned him to his kingdom, and we had something else for supper.

Now and then, when Mom could catch us and get us all cleaned up, we went to the Methodist Sunday school in Hull.

June and I had a colored Bible picture book, which June would read to me on occasions. Sometimes I sat and looked at the pictures by myself. I especially liked the picture of Jesus and the little children, but I was puzzled by the caption, "Suffer the little children and forbid them not to come unto me." Having seen a picture of Jesus on the cross my little girl mind told me that if I went to Sunday school, I would have to "suffer" as Jesus did.

Each time I looked at that picture book, the scarier the thought of attending Sunday school became. Finally I had to ask Mom about it, and she assured me that going to Sunday school to learn about Jesus didn't mean that I would have to suffer.

I couldn't talk June into playing dolls with me very often. She was definitely an outdoor girl who favored building tramp traps on the levee with Bill over playing dolls with me.

Tramp traps were products of June and Bill's inventive and ingenious minds. Mom and Dad warned us that if a ragged stranger came around the farm, we should run to our parents or one of the older kids, because the person could be dangerous. The possibility of a visit from a hobo or a tramp did exist, but June and Bill took it a little more seriously than I did.

They dug holes along the sand levee and covered them with willow limbs. Sometimes they waited behind cotton wood trees for a glimpse of their intended prey. Usually, though, they made a daily tramp-trap-run along the levee. They never did catch a single vagrant, but they considered their work a worthy endeavor.

During my small growing up years, the three boys taught their two little sisters something that Mom would probably have left out of our education had she known the lesson was in progress. They showed us how to broomstraw a horse fly. It was a simple process which yielded spectacular results.

First, we chose the biggest horsefly we could catch. We were blessed or cursed, depending on the viewpoint, with an abundance of subjects, so making this selection presented no problem. Next, we culled a slender broomstraw from Mom's porch broom, trimming it to a length of two or three inches.

Finally, grasping the horsefly firmly in the left hand and holding it hind-side before, we quickly added the straw to its anatomy. Then we let it fly. The addition of the straw to the insect's flying gear created an imbalance which caused his flight pattern to follow a most bizarre path.

After the onset of the Second World War, we equated the zigzagging horseflies with enemy fighter planes. Each careening fly became a disabled enemy plane spiraling through the sky to a certain and most deserved death.

It seemed a logical analogy. To us, riding a horse which was under attack from horseflies could be as dangerous as flying a bomber plane. Therefore, instigating a counter attack, whatever the battle strategy, was worthwhile.

Bill was Dad's shadow, so when the truck left the lot, Bill was usually in it. One hot windy summer day Dad had to make a quick trip into town. "Can I go, Dad? Please, please," he begged. "I'll wait in the truck I won't get in your way."

"No, Bill, you can't go this time. I'll tell you what, though. When I get back, you can help me tear down that shed between the big fuel tank and the front yard gate. Then we'll burn the lumber."

Bill followed Dad down the flagstone walk and through the gate making one last attempt to get in on the trip to town. Dad left him standing at the gate next to the doomed shed.

June and I strolled out to the gate. "Come on, Bill. Let's play," we urged.

"Naw, I'm gonna get rid of this shed for Dad." Mom called us back into the house to dry the dishes. I followed Mom, but June chose to stay with Bill.

I was standing by the cupboard drying knives and forks when Mom asked, "What's that smell? Is something burning somewhere?" She looked out the kitchen window. "Oh, my, oh, my! Billie's burning the shed down! Patsie, stay in the house! Garnette, go get Johnnie and Dickie. They're out at the hog lot. June! Billie! Get in this house!" Mom grabbed the dishpan and raced to the burning shed. "Look out! Look out!" she shouted, dousing the shed with the water from the pan.

I followed her outside. "Get back," she warned, swishing her apron at me. "The fuel tank may blow up!"

Johnnie and Dick came running. They offered to throw water on the burning building, but Mom ordered them into the house. Just as quickly as the old tar-papered building flamed, the fire burned out, leaving the fuel tank still standing intact.

"Boy, you're gonna get it when Dad gets home," Johnnie

and Dick warned Bill. But when Dad saw the charred ruins of the old shed and found that nobody was burned, his face registered relief.

"Bill, the next time you decide to help me burn a building, wait until I get there. You could've hurt yourself and a lot of other people."

We almost always went to bed just shortly past sundown. During the summer months that was fine, but in winter we'd often be in bed by seven o'clock in the evening. This rule worked for Garnette, June, and me, but sometimes the three boys had a little too much energy to go to bed quite that early. Often they engaged in some harmless wrestling before slipping off to dreamland.

However, Dad had different ideas about how they should use that excess vim and verve. When the crashes and thumps and muffled giggles got out of control, he went to the bottom of the stairs and called, "You boys get dressed and go throw some hay down for the cattle. It'll give you a head start on tomorrow's chores."

"We'll quit, Dad, honest."

It was always the same — Dad's order followed by the boys' promise to quit. But Dad never gave in. He never honored the promise with a reply.

As the boys dressed and hurried down the stairs, small arguing always began. "You started it."

"Did not. Dick threw his pillow first."

"No, I didn't."

It was usually about here that I could hear the kitchen door close softly, and I knew that the cows and the boys would be fine in the morning.

So went our lives on the farm near the river. Dad drank a little too much whiskey now and then, and sometimes Mom lost her temper when he did. But for the most part, life was good.

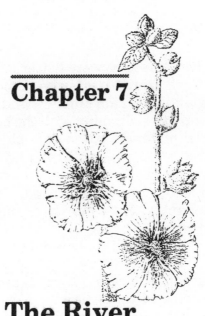

Chapter 7

The River

The face of the water, in time became a wonderful book...not...to be read once and thrown aside, for it had a new story to tell every day.

"Life on the Mississippi"

On a map it was the Mississippi. To us, it was always and simply "the river." Most of the time, the river was predictable. A common part of our daily lives, it ambled along its deep, silted channel, providing fish for our table and a respite from summer's heat for youthful swimmers. But each time heavy spring rains swelled rolling waters to the levee top, causing seep water to spread over acres of new crops, a profound appreciation of its power reasserted itself in the mind.

Mom raised most of her 13 children within a quarter mile of the river — a biting irony since she had an intense fear of water. Any body of water large enough to harm one of her kids bothered my protective and instinctive mother. So the sloughs and the horse tank took second place to the river only because of their size — they were still water. Because of this, an unspoken agreement amongst all of her kids (except me — I shared her dislike of water) prevailed. Water stories, especially river episodes, were better left untold.

Because June learned to swim almost as early as she learned to walk, she couldn't understand Mom's fear of water. "June, you can't go swimming with the boys and that's final," Mom told the pigtailed, seven-year-old one warm summer day. The three boys had gone to their favorite swimming hole without inviting her.

"I'd just like to know why I can't go," June insisted, folding her arms defiantly across her chest and stamping her bare foot on the floor.

"Because the boys will be swimming without their clothes on."

"I don't care! I don't care! I want to swim, too!" Swimming sans clothes was not the issue with June; swimming was the issue. She loved to swim. Mom hated water. So for that reason and, of course, because the boys were going skinny dipping, June lost the argument. The seep water slough that ran near the north side of the yard became her swimming spot for the afternoon, and I tagged along. Mom could get from her kitchen to the slough in a split-second if we needed help.

Another day I took my doll to the cool, shady south porch and attempted to lull her to sleep in the porch swing. My plaintive lullaby was interrupted by a commotion in the barn lot. I ran into the yard in time to see Dick hurry through the gate and run for the pond in the south pasture. At that same moment, I heard Bill call to Mom from the slough, "He's not here."

Mom raced to the big horse tank which stood next to the pump in the lot and thrust her arm shoulder deep into its greenish depths. No matter what the circumstance, if one of Mom's kids came up missing, she always ran for the horse tank. But today's search, like all previous horse tank searches, yielded no half-drowned child. "John-neee," she called, now in a fit of desperation, "where are you?" Dick ran back from the pond.

"He's not out there, Mom. The water's not even been stirred up at all."

Mom hurried back to the yard near the opened cellar door

where I was standing. "John-neee," she called again. "Patsie, have you seen Johnnie?"

"I'm right here, Mom. What's all the fuss about?" Johnnie climbed up out of the cellar. Mom had left the large, four by six-foot door open early that morning "to air the mustiness out of the place."

"I've been sittin' on the cellar steps, thinkin'; it's cool down there," Johnnie explained.

Mom pulled her missing boy close and hugged him. "Is that where you've been? I thought you fell in the horse tank or the slough! Next time, let me know where you're going so I won't get so scared." She grabbed him by the shoulders and affected a stern shake.

A neighbor lady, six miles down the levee, often went swimming with her seven sons. Mom couldn't believe it. One day, when some of the older kids in our family came back from swimming with the Kroenckes, the report came back to Mom: "Mrs. Kroencke sure is a good swimmer. She went to the river with us today."

Mom was shocked. "Charlie, did you know that Mrs. Kroencke puts on a bathing suit and swims with her boys?"

"Sure, Corrie," Dad teased, "you should try it. I bet you'd enjoy swimming."

"Hmph! I don't think women who are mothers should wear bathing suits." Mom grasped her apron on the sides and gave it that familiar swish. "You won't see me in a bathing suit," the proper lady stated with an indignant air.

Mom's worries about the river started soon after the move to Pike County. Wilbur and Clyde lost no time in exploring the wonders of skinny dipping in the mighty Mississippi River. When Uncle Frank and Aunt Susie came down, the two boys shared their discoveries with our visiting cousin, Jack.

The three bib overall clad boys raced through the south yard gate and across the pasture to the river. They stepped out of their shoes at the pasture-side base of the levee. Hot, sunscorched, burr-filled sand demanded quick, lively steps up and over the levee. Bibs were unbuckled during the

downside trip and dropped at the water's edge where the
clear, cool, exhilarating river welcomed the hot, naked swimmers.

Two small islands lay between the boys and the sound of a
steam-powered, paddle-wheel excursion boat. Agility and
familiarity with the paths the river had carved for itself soon
found the three boys at the main channel edge of the second
island in full view of the boat.

A combination of summer innocence and boyish mis-
chievousness gave the passengers of the boat an unexpected
picture of life on the Mississippi. The three daring skinny
dippers pulled themselves from the water and stood in all
their dripping, sun-tanned glory, waving exuberantly to the
onlookers.

"Boys," Wilbur suggested as they walked toward home in
the shadows of the summer evening, "don't say anything to
Mom about waving at the paddle-wheeler. I think it would
make her mad."

The three little boys learned about skinny dipping in the
river, too. Dad threw them from a log into the river, thus
introducing them to swimming. They loved it. As soon as
their slick, wet heads popped up from the water, they swam
back to the log, begging to be tossed in again. They learned
something else about skinny dipping. They learned to hang
their bibs in the shade of the tree-lined river's edge. Metal
buttons and hooks burned at the touch when left in the direct
sun.

The boys and June learned something about the winter
river that Mom wouldn't hear of until all four were married
with children of their own.

Early in life, Dad taught the boys to respect a gun. He
stressed extreme caution while hunting. Because June could
be found with Dad as often as she was with Mom, Garnette,
or me, she learned the lessons about guns and hunting, too.
Hunting was not done for sport; it was done for food. And so
a hunting expedition consisting of Dick, Johnnie, Bill, and
June was not unusual, with the seriousness of the event
being understood by all concerned.

When a particularly cold winter day caused Mom to comment that fried rabbits and gravy would be good for supper, the four kids were on their way. They headed toward the river levee where a growth of underbrush promised enough rabbits for a good meal. Dick carried the gun.

The pasture side of the underbrush yielded no rabbits, so the happy little foursome crossed the levee and headed toward the first of the two islands which separated them from the main channel of the river. Crossing over to the island was easy, because the shallow off-shoot from the river was frozen solid.

Since it was easy to get to the first island, one of the kids suggested that the second island would certainly contain the biggest rabbits. Again, the frozen water between the islands provided easy access to their destination.

The river side of the second island offered quite a surprise to the brave hunters. Undercurrents in the main channel had created a spectacular ice jam.

Great sheets and blocks of ice, haphazardly tumbled together and wedged into a frozen wonderland by unpredictable forces far down in the depths of the river, captured the imaginations of the adventurers.

"Let's go climb on them," suggested June, oblivious to any danger. Maybe to prove their masculinity or perhaps because the challenge was too inviting, the three boys agreed, and all four kids crawled out onto the jagged, icy wonderland. But their enjoyment was short lived.

"Help me! Help me!" Johnnie's voice could be heard, but no brave little ice climber could be seen.

"Where are you, Johnnie?" Dick called back, still holding the hunting gun.

"Here he is, Dick," Bill called. "He fell in a hole."

Dick and June crawled across the slippery, jagged terrain toward Bill and the sound of Johnnie's desperate call. Great chunks of stubborn ice, none of which had yielded to the others created an ice pocket into which Johnnie had fallen. Just the top of his head was visible.

"Help me out, boys, please." Fear gripped the trapped child.

Grasping the edge of his prison in an effort to pull himself up, he fell backwards — his hands filled with crumbled ice.

"Dick, Dick, are you still there?"

"We're here, Johnnie. We'll get you out."

Dick gathered Bill and June close to him. "Lay down on the ice," he ordered. "June, hold real tight to Bill's feet. Bill, you grab my ankles and hold on as tight as you can. I'm gonna hand the gun down to Johnnie and then you kids pull as hard as you can."

The frightened little chain of bodies pulled their brother to freedom. "Let's go home," June declared. She had had enough of the icy wonderland. But they were to have one more trial before they would sit next to the warm stove in the kitchen drinking Mom's hot cocoa.

As they started across the ice between them and the river levee, a long, ominous cracking sound broke the winter stillness. "The ice is going, kids, run!" Johnnie shouted. The three boys were across the ice and headed toward the levee when they realized that June was not with them.

"Wait for me," they heard. Behind them, crawling cautiously across the expanse of cracking ice, came June. "It cracks when I walk. I'm afraid. Come and get me."

"Don't stop, June. You're just about to shore. Keep crawling," the boys ordered as they ran back down the levee toward their stranded sister. The three boys got to her just as she crawled onto the shore. Together they raced toward the levee and headed for home, far away from the eerie, cracking sounds of thawing ice.

"No rabbits?" Mom asked as she poured hot cocoa for the hunters and me.

"Naw. Too cold. Must be up the other way," the kids mumbled.

"You must have had a good time, anyway. You've been gone quite awhile."

"We played on the ice for awhile," June offered.

Mom frowned.

Dick, Johnnie, and Bill gave June a warning look, and nothing more was said about it.

In 1942, the destructive might of the Mississippi made itself known to everyone in the broad valley. Heavy spring rains raised the river well beyond flood level, causing its muddy waters to lap dangerously close to the levee top. Land varmints, whose habit it was to burrow deep nesting holes into the sides of the levee, along with the constant motion of the relentless water, further weakened the dike. A break would have caused total destruction to us and our neighbors for miles up and down the river. Run-off water from the hills north of us and seep water from the swollen river flooded our farm. Dad moved us out.

After renting a three-room house near Plainville, Dad and the boys loaded absolute necessities onto our spring wagon and deposited us in our temporary home. Not quite realizing the seriousness of the situation, I enjoyed the entire adventure.

Dad and my brothers who were old enough walked the levee. Along with all our neighbors, they took their turn patrolling and carrying sandbags to low or weak areas. The work was not in vain. The levee remained intact — the river stayed in place. When the rains finally abated and the seep water dissipated, we moved back home.

The seep water had not gotten into our home or our outbuildings, but it did destroy most of the spring crops. Life went on and a beguiling summer river flowed by our house, once more a source of fun, but never again to be completely trusted.

Chapter 8

A Fizzled Fourth

*One of the most striking differences between a cat
and a lie is that a cat has only nine lives.*

"Pudd'nhead Wilson's Calendar"

I was only four when it all happened, but the events must
have been traumatic. I sure do remember.

July 4, 1940 started nice enough. Ruby brought some
girlfriends home from Peoria. On the way down to our house,
they stopped in Hull and bought two cases of soda pop, the
first June and I had ever tasted.

Dad, Clyde, and Wilbur bought a box of fireworks. "Don't
touch these 'til it turns dark," Dad warned. With homemade
ice cream and a bottle of the wonderful new taste sensation,
soda pop, we managed to wait till the sun went down. "Only
one bottle of pop 'til time for fireworks," Dad cautioned.

I had a pet calico cat that summer. Vanity got the best of
me when I overheard Ruby's Peoria girlfriends saying, "Your
baby sister sure is cute. She looks so darling carrying that
big calico cat around."

Mom had dressed June and me in special summer dresses
for the festivities. I had found a wide, pink ribbon and tied it

around my cat's neck to compliment my regalia. The cat's bow matched the ribbons on my pigtails.

"Patsie, take that ribbon off your cat," Dad demanded. "That's an animal, and animals should not have ribbons around their necks. They could get caught in the brush and strangle."

"All right, I will in a minute," I agreed. But instead, I carried the cat outside and sat next to Mom's roses.

Comments such as "Don't you two look cute," "Does anybody have a camera?" and "Patsie and her cat look just like a picture," inflated my ego to dangerous proportions.

"What does Dad know about cats and ribbons?" I thought. "Everybody thinks I look cute." I spent most of the afternoon lugging around my ribbon bedecked cat and drinking from the intoxicating, addictive bottle of self-pride.

June and Bill deftly slipped an extra bottle of soda pop from the wooden case and hid behind the wash house. They took turns sipping the wonderful, bubbly new drink. They paid no heed to Dad's warning about drinking too much soda; I paid no heed to his edict about the cat's ribbon. Dad, busy with our company, didn't check to see if we had carried out his orders.

Pauline and Todd were there with Tommy and Terry, their two toddlers. Opal and Dode brought their little girls, Shirley and Dixie, who were close in ages to Todd's boys. Farm talk and enjoyment of grandchildren drew Dad's attention from his own three misbehaving offspring.

At last darkness settled over farm and fields. "I'll light the fireworks," Wilbur volunteered.

My intrepid brother carried the box of fireworks over by a trough which he had leaned against the south yard fence. He set one of the rockets in the trough, explaining that it would zoom out over the pasture toward the pond.

Clyde wanted in on the launching. He impetuously struck a match and held it against the fuse on a rocket.

"No, Clyde, wait!" Wilbur's warning came too late. He hadn't had time to move the fireworks box. In an instant flames were shooting everywhere. Exploding strings of fire crackers cavorted and popped wildly through the grass. Lazy, sputtering sparks of blue and red poured from Roman candles and died. Rockets screamed through the air in all directions.

Pauline and Opal scooped up their toddlers and hurried onto the porch. In less than five minutes, our entire box of fireworks had erupted in a somewhat less than spectacular display of zooming, fizzling, and spitting disappointment. My cat was gone in less time than that. The first misdirected rocket had sent her running for cover.

Mom worried that a rocket might go down the chimney and cause a fire, but it didn't happen. June, Bill, and I worried that the soda pop bottles might be shattered by a rocket, but that didn't happen either. Dad poured a bucket of water on the smoldering fireworks box, and our Fourth of July was over for that year. But at least none of us got hurt.

We helped pick up the debris, washed our feet in the foot tub on the porch, and went to bed.

But the evening was still young for Ruby and her three friends. They all piled into the Peoria girls' car and drove over to Hannibal.

"Ruby, what's a good place to get a coke and dance to some good jukebox music?" Babe, Ruby's friend, asked.

"I really don't know," Ruby answered. "I really haven't been in Hannibal all that often."

"There's a sign. Pull in there," one of the girls offered, pointing to a flashing CocaCola sign on the front of a building. The youthful foursome entered the dimly lit "restaurant." A jukebox was blaring in the back.

Only one long, oval-shaped table surrounded by about a dozen chairs furnished the room. A waitress took the girls' orders. A young man came up and asked one of Ruby's friends to dance and she accepted.

"What kind of a place is this, Ruby? Have you been here before?" asked Nora, Ruby's friend.

"No, I never have, but it sure is dirty, isn't it?" Ruby laughed nervously and glanced around the room. Four door-ways decorated with dingy, gaudy drapes caught her eye. The rumpled head and torso of a young woman appeared from behind a beaded drape and stared back at her.

"Wha'cha doin' here, Honey?" the hard-looking young woman asked, laughing at Ruby. Suddenly my almost too innocent sister realized her plight.

"Nora," she whispered to one of her friends, "let's all get out of here. I know where we are!"

Abruptly the girls left the "restaurant" and jumped into their car. "Step on it, Babe," Ruby demanded. "That was a... we just came from a... Mom calls them 'houses of ill repute.'"

"Oh, no, Ruby, we didn't..." All four girls dissolved in a puddle of giggles as they drove back to our house as fast as they could.

"For gosh sakes, don't tell Mom and Dad or any of the kids where we've been," Ruby warned. "I don't think Mom would let me go back to Peoria if she knew the blunder I just made."

The next morning an unusually quiet group ate pancakes at our breakfast table. "Did you girls have a good time last night?" Dad asked.

The girls exchanged knowing glances. "Oh, yes, Mr. Dunker," Babe answered, "but we were tired so we just grabbed a CocaCola and came right back."

"Hannibal's a nice town, but we don't go over there very much," Dad continued.

"Dad, the girls would like to go horseback riding today," Ruby interrupted. She wanted nothing more than to pull the discussion away from the events of last night.

"All right. I'll go catch the horses while you girls help do up the breakfast dishes."

Dad left and the girls began to giggle about the night before. I listened in enough to understand that they had been someplace that they didn't want Mom and Dad to know about and then the conversation became uninteresting. I decided to go outside and watch Dad ready the horses for our visiting city girls.

As I stepped onto the porch I remembered my calico cat. I hadn't seen it since the big fireworks "display" of the night before.

"Here, kitty, kitty," I called, but to no avail. I was standing out behind the house looking up into the sycamore tree when Dad called to me.

"Patsie Ellen, get out here," he ordered in a very stern tone. Dad was standing next to the peach tree in the southeast corner of the yard. "Did you take the ribbon off your cat last night?" he asked.

"N...no," I stammered.

"I know you didn't, young lady and the very thing that I told you could happen, did happen. I found your cat in the peach tree. The ribbon caught on a limb and he hung himself. I've already buried him." Dad looked at me with sad eyes. I'm sorry, Patsie, but I hope this is a lesson to you."

So ended the Fourth of July, 1940 — not with a bang, not with a sparkle, but with a fithzz.

Chapter 9

Slick Blue

"...Cast your eye on me, gentlemen! and lay low and hold your breath, for I'm 'bout to turn myself loose!"

"Adventures of Huckleberry Finn"

From the time my memory first began to serve me, I remember breakfast and Slick Blue. Mom fixed pancakes every morning, and we chased Slick Blue every chance we got. Dad tossed the pancakes to outstretched waiting plates, and we caught them, but we never caught Slick Blue.

Dad expected perfect attendance at the breakfast table unless illness intervened. When all the chairs around our big kitchen table were filled, Mom brought two heaping platters of pancakes from the warming oven on the stove and placed them in front of Dad for tossing. He would pick up a platter and toss the cakes frisbee style until he emptied the platter, and then he tossed from the second one. Dick, Johnnie, and Bill competed to see who could eat the most. Bill ate ten one morning. I never could see how he did it because Mom served fried potatoes, bacon, ham, eggs, and green onions in season along with her pancakes, and Bill helped himself to some of everything. I do know that nobody ever topped his record.

Breakfast served as information time. We discussed events for the coming day and took orders for specific jobs. Breakfast reports about our married siblings kept us in touch with those who had moved away.

The whereabouts of Slick Blue was a common breakfast topic among us kids, especially during the spring and summer months. Slick Blue was a cat, but he was no ordinary feline. This muscular, steel-blue tomcat had been seen sneaking around our barns and corn crib for about three years, leaving dead litters of baby kittens and empty pigeon nests in his wake.

Slick Blue's coat matched that of my latest kitten. I realized that the obvious similarity was no happenstance; the ornery, marauding tomcat was the father of my pet. This knowledge raised a tiny spot of compassion in my heart. Because my pet was so sweet and gentle, I knew that his father couldn't be all bad.

I didn't dare tell June and the boys how I felt. No self-respecting Dunker kid could like Slick Blue. Still, at first I was secretly glad that Mom rarely, if ever, let me go on any of the hunts for the infamous cat. Glad, that is, until he ate the babies from the nest of our pet pigeon, Bill.

Bill was a great pigeon. He flew down to anyone who tapped his shoulder and called, "Come, Bill, come sit on my shoulder." One day when Garnette was serving as Bill's perch, he laid an egg. So we called him "Billy." We thought that sounded more feminine.

Anyway, one morning at breakfast Dad announced, "Girls, I have a surprise to show you in the barn. As soon as you get these dishes done, come and get me and I'll show it to you."

That morning the dishes got washed and put away in record time. Mom had a way of making dish washing go quickly when a special circumstance warranted.

"Dad, where are you?" We were out in the lot and headed for the barn. "Where's the surprise? The dishes are done."

Dad came toward us from the hog lot. "I haven't checked on them yet this morning, but wait 'til you see what I found last night."

He led us to a protected corner of the barn. The mangled bodies of five, dead, baby kittens were strewn in a nest of hay. "Oh-h-h," Dad moaned, "they were all alive last night." A quick check in the nest of our pet pigeon told the same story; a predator had been in the barn.

Instantly realizing how the baby kittens had been destroyed and what steps would have to be taken, June stated, "Slick Blue did it, Dad. I'll go get the three boys." The summer's chase began.

I wanted in on it this time, but Mom wouldn't let me. The boys didn't want me either. The only reason they allowed June to join in the chase for the infamous cat was because she could crawl under the corn crib without getting stuck.

Intermittent tomcat chases usually lasted for two or three days at a time all summer, but the picket gate in the front yard fence served as my vantage point for keeping up with the proceedings. Any given chase found me squinting through the slats, cheering the warriors and offering cat location information to anyone who would listen. Two or three days after we found the dead kittens, the first major Slick Blue chase ended with the cat claiming the victory. As was his wont, he disappeared.

Mom's breakfast table announcement drew our attention from the lost battle. "Opal and Pauline are both due to get new babies real soon so Todd and Pauline's little boys, Tommy and Terry, and Opal and Dode's little girls, Shirley, and Dixie are going to stay with us. You'll all have to help out."

As we washed and dried the breakfast dishes that day, June and I tried to decide who would sleep where when our nieces and nephews arrived. Our discussion was interrupted by "the call."

"Slick Blue's back!" Johnnie shouted from the front yard gate. June and I raced outside.

"Come on, Bill," June coaxed the usually willing tomcat chaser. "Let's go get him."

"Naw, I don't feel good. I'm going in the house."

Bill moped into the house and flopped down on the cot in the living room. His apathy toward Slick Blue was so unusual that it prompted Mom to assess the situation immediately. Thus began our whooping cough siege. Bill wasn't very sick with the disease, but he sure passed it around.

A few days later, June came down with a fever. Mom diagnosed whooping cough again. Like Bill, June had a mild case of the aggravating malady, and both kids were over it by the time Todd and Dode brought their little kids.

On the first day of June, Todd drove up the lane with four-year-old Tommy and two-and-a-half-year-old Terry. "The boys aren't feeling very good, Mom," he said as he brought his sons and their clothes into the kitchen. "But Pauline isn't feeling too good either, so I brought the boys now, in case the baby comes tonight."

Neither Pauline nor Opal had planned to deliver in the hospital. This decision was neither unusual nor inconvenient unless, of course, whooping cough entered the picture. That turn of events could complicate matters, and it did.

Dode drove into the lot just as Todd was leaving. He brought five-year-old Shirley and three-year-old Dixie, both of whom were well into the beginning throes of whooping cough.

"Opal's not feeling too good today, Mom, so I brought the girls on down. I think we're going to be getting that new baby any time, now."

Mom and Garnette pulled the roll-away bed into the living room and opened it out. Mom also put sheets on the cot, and our living room became a hospital for the four coughing grandchildren. I succumbed to the disease that same day.

Earlier that same spring, Pearl and Karl and their six-year-old daughter, Nancy, had moved from Peoria to a farm just two miles north of us. When the whooping cough epidemic hit, Pearl came down to help Mom and Garnette. Nancy got sick along with the rest of us. For two weeks Mom's living room hospital housed six whooping kids, all under seven.

Terry and Dixie were the sickest. Each time a coughing

spasm erupted, these two little patients nearly strangled before freeing the choking mucous from their systems.

Mom and Garnette scrubbed and disenfected the slop jars every day and set them at the foot of each bed. The reservoir on the kitchen cookstove supplied countless gallons of hot water for the extra bedding that had to be washed — sometimes twice a day.

Through it all, life went on. Mom fixed pancakes for breakfast every morning. Even though she had six patients in her makeshift hospital requiring bland diets, she still had Dad, Clyde, Garnette, Dick, Johnnie, Bill, and June who were healthy and hungry.

The first morning that I was proclaimed well enough to go out on the porch to play, Slick Blue returned. How I envied June as I watched her race out to the lot and join in on the chase.

"Did you get him?" June and Bill had come back to the porch after the chase, and I was anxious to hear what happened.

"Naw," Bill answered, "he took out for the truck patch the last I saw of him."

By the middle of June, everybody had gone home. Terry and Tommy joined their new baby sister, Phyllis, and Shirley and Dixie welcomed a baby brother, Larry. The two new grandchildren were born only three days apart.

That same month Wilbur joined the Air Force and some of the sparkle left Mom's disposition. Dad's patience grew shorter than usual. Every day we would see them huddled close to our table-top radio, gleaning what war news they could from the crackling static of reports from overseas.

Only one thing remained constant in our lives — the anticipation of the next "Slick Blue chase."

Chapter 10

Mouse Pies and a Mystery

Courage is resistance to fear, mastery of fear — not absence of fear.

"Pudd'nhead Wilson's Calendar"

"Mexicali Rose, stop crying,
I'll come back to you some sunny day;
Every hour the day you know I'm pining,
every hour the day while I'm away.
Dry those big brown eyes and smile dear,
vanish all those tears and please don't cry;
Mexicali Rose, I'm leaving, Mexicali Rose, Good-bye."

Peachy Thomas leaned on the long handle of his corn scoop and listened as my six-year-old voice warbled this sad lament. I was perched on my shelf in the corner of the red slatted corn crib.

Peachy worked for the local grain elevator. When Dad had corn to sell, Peachy showed up. I loved his visits. I knew he'd sing songs with us and tell us mouse pie stories. I believed that his mother made mouse pies because he said she did. And when a cow gave birth to a calf — I really believed that she dug it up out in the pasture because Dad said she did.

One day I followed Dad out to the pasture to see a new calf. "Where'd the cow get her calf, Dad?" I asked.

"She dug it up out here."

Dad said it; it was true. Peachy said his mom made mouse pies; it was true.

That's the kind of kid I was. I rarely questioned anything. For example, the shelf I sat on when I sang. I never reasoned that a corn crib didn't need shelves and that my shelf was nothing more than a support brace.

"Yessirree, kids," Peachy would say to the youngest Dunkers, "Ma usta have me'n muh brother ketch all the mice we could hold in both hands, 'specially 'em baby 'uns, and she'd make us a big ole mouse pie fer supper. You young'uns orta ketch some mice fer yore ma. I jes' betcha she'd bake a mouse pie fer you jes' like my ma did fer muh brother'n me."

I could just imagine Mom making a mouse pie! Why, you couldn't get within a mile of her if you were carrying a mouse. She felt about mice the same way she felt about bugs. Once I found some baby mice and put them in a match box to show her. I did that only once.

Well, anyway, I was sitting on my shelf watching Peachy scoop corn and believing every word he was saying when I heard the three boys, talking about the bay horse.

"Yes, he did," Dick argued. "He traded the jersey heifer with the new calf for that big old bay of old Joe McDole's and McDole threw in a half acre of stump potatoes. I guess you guys know who'll have to dig the potatoes."

"I'll dig potatoes," said Bill, "but I sure hope I don't have to ride that old horse home."

"Why not?" Dick asked.

"Because he's mean, that's why."

"Oh, how do you know?"

"I just know, that's how."

"Oh, he's not mean." Johnnie was the stabilizer. He always tried to help Dick and Bill reach an agreement before a full-blown argument got started. "You're just making that up, Bill."

"No, I'm not. I heard Dad say that the bay would be a good

work horse if we could take some of the orneriness out of him."

I knew Dick was hoping that Bill was "just making that up" because Dick knew and I knew who would be riding the bay horse home.

"I'm not afraid to ride that horse home," Dick stated. I wasn't too sure that Dick actually believed what he had just said, but he wasn't going to admit it to Bill.

"It's a good thing because it's eighty miles to old Joe McDole's and that twisty, old, rutty road along the Sny is all grown up thick with willows on both sides." The Sny was a wide deep waterway which served as a natural drainage channel for river seep water. It was a good place to catch fish, but the boys weren't thinking of fishing today.

I was beginnig to worry. I climbed down from my shelf and stepped outside. I leaned against the crib and listened to the discussion. I had never been to the McDole farm. If the road to that farm was eighty miles long and lined with willows on both sides as Bill had said, I figured it must be a terrible place to go.

That night, after supper, we took Dick to get the horse. "You might as well ride along, Corrie," Dad said to Mom. "I'm just taking Dick over to get the bay horse I traded for. We'll be right back."

"I think I will. Do you want to come with us, Patsie?"

I really didn't want to go. I didn't even want them to go. I didn't understand how they could take Dick that far away from home and leave him to ride a mean horse back. How did they know if Dick even knew the way back? Had anybody even asked Dick if he wanted to ride the horse home?

I wanted to ask Dad all these questions, but I knew him well enough to know that it wouldn't do me any good to question his judgment. Not too many people argued much with my dad. *But Bill said the load was long and twisty and filled with ruts and holes,* I thought. *Bill said it so it must be true. He wouldn't make up a story like that.* I couldn't understand why Dad didn't know what Bill knew about the road. Dad picked me up and set me on the seat of the truck between him and Mom. Dick climbed into the back.

Bill was right. The road to Joe McDole's was eighty miles long (at least it seemed that far to me) and so full of ruts and holes that I could hardly stay on the truck seat. Poor Dick. I was afraid that we were going to throw him right out of the back of the truck.

Bill was right about the willow trees, too. They were thick - and endless. *What if that old bay horse gets scared by a rabbit or something and runs off into those willows? Why, we'll never find Dick in that brush.* My imagination was going strong.

"You're a quiet little girl tonight, Patsie. What are you thinking so hard about?" Dad's voice interrupted my thoughts. I just sat there. I didn't try to answer. *Dick's my brother!* I thought. *I may never see him again after tonight.* I couldn't explain to Dad how I felt because I knew he wouldn't understand, and because we had just pulled up to the McDole barn.

Silently I prayed, "Please, oh, please make Joe McDole tell my dad that he doesn't want to trade his old bay horse for my dad's cow and calf." But to no avail.

Mr. McDole strolled over toward the truck. "Howdy, Charlie. Reckon you've come fer tha' bay?"

"Sure have, Joe. Hop out of the truck, Dick. Here's your horse."

Mom and I waited in the truck. I climbed onto her lap to get a better view of things (and to get a more secure feeling). I looked up at the tallest horse I'd ever seen.

"He spooks a little 'round strangers, Son," Mr. McDole was saying to Dick, "but don't be a skeered of 'im 'cause he usely only does it jest onct."

Dad gave Dick a foot up onto the horse. As soon as Dick straddled the tall animal's back, that old bay gave out with the loudest squeal I'd ever heard. He didn't whinny like a real horse; he squealed. Then he reared straight up, his front legs flailing the air. Dick hung on.

I hid my face in Mom's apron. I could see that Bill was right about the horse. He was mean. Now I knew for sure that Dick would never make it back home.

"You don't have to be afraid, Patsie. Look, the horse is already trotting right down the road, just as calm as you please. If your dad doesn't hurry, Dickie will beat us home."

I sat on Mom's lap with my face hidden in her apron and I cried. *Didn't Mom know?* I thought. *Didn't she understand that the old Sny road was eighty miles long and lined on both sides with willows that grew very close together and made the road dark and lonesome? Hadn't she paid any attention when we brought Dick here?*

Dad climbed back into the truck. "What's going on here? What's the matter with you, Patsie?"

"Oh, she's afraid for Dickie," Mom answered him.

"He's going to be fine. You don't have to worry. Corrie, I'm going to take the field road home because I want to check those potatoes."

I couldn't believe my ears. Dick was probably totally lost and we were going to take the time to check some dumb old potatoes that some old man had planted in a half acre of stumps. *They probably aren't any good at all,* I thought. *I'll bet Dad didn't make a very good trade this time.*

We bumped along the field road to a place where Mr. McDole had cleared some young trees and planted a bushel of seed potatoes. Dad pulled up a plant and held out for Mom to see. Hanging from the roots were three or four good-sized potatoes. "Oughta' be some big ones in the ground," he called to us as he pulled another plant. Laying the potatoes at Mom's feet, Dad said, "Well, I guess I'll send the boys over here tomorrow if it don't rain. I think they're ready, don't you?"

Mom agreed with Dad and we rode home in silence. My parents were obviously enjoying the quiet summer drive while I, on the other hand, was miserable. The minute Dad pulled the truck up to the front yard fence, I jumped off Mom's lap and out of the truck, heading straight for the lane. Just as I had feared, no Dick.

The tears which I had managed to check somewhat during the ride home, ran freely again. Dad strolled out across the lot to the end of the lane and stopped beside me.

Together, we watched for Dick — Dad with full knowledge that a boy on a horse would soon be silhouetted against the evening sky and me with Bill's words ringing in my ears, *He's a mean horse and it's eighty miles to old Joe McDole's house.*

Dad pointed toward the far end of the lane. "Look, Patsie, you can stop crying now." He was losing his patience, "Here they come."

Sure enough, Dick had found his way home. I watched him rein the new horse around the corner and down our lane. And I could tell that he was enjoying himself as he confidently coaxed the tall horse into a brisk trot.

I learned something that day. I learned that I could trust my brothers about a lot of things, but not about how far it was to Joe McDole's. And I learned that Dick wasn't as fearful about his ride as I was. As a matter of fact, I learned that Dick was quite adept at handling horses.

During November of that same year, Dick took a ride with a team of horses that was far more exciting than the ride from Joe McDole's.

"It was just plain weird." That's what Dick said about it.

Dad had invited friends from Peoria to come down and do some duck hunting. Mom, too, enjoyed seeing old friends and was happy to be fixing them a special dinner when Clyde came bursting through the kitchen door. He was soaking wet and breathless.

"Mom, Mom, Mom, I, I ..." His face was white. He was obviously extremely frightened.

"What on earth is wrong, Clyde? Are you sick?" Mom led him to a chair. "Here, sit down and catch your breath."

Clyde fell into the chair.

"River, river," he began, pointing toward the river. "I found a... There's a man..."

"You're all right, now, Clyde. Did the man chase you? Did he threaten you?"

"No, no, Mom, he's, he's dead! I've been out hunting for the new calf. When I saw the man's heel in the brush, I thought it was the calf's foot. I thought the calf had drowned so I went down to pull him out, only it wasn't the calf, it was a person, a dead person." Clyde began to shiver.

"How did you get so wet, Clyde?" Mom began to help him unbutton his coat.

"I must've run through some water somewhere — I don't know."

"Well, go change out of those wet clothes and I'll get your Dad," Mom ordered.

Our place became a hubbub of activity. Dad drove into town and called the sheriff. Then he drove down to Todd and Pauline's and brought Todd to our house. Nobody was allowed to go down to the levee to view the gruesome find.

When the sheriff arrived, he and his deputies, along with Dad and Todd, went over to the river. "You boys hitch the team to the spring wagon and drive it on over to the spot where you found the body," Dad said to Clyde and Dick. "Todd and I will go on with the sheriff, but he'll be needing to talk with you, Clyde, so hurry."

Clyde wasn't too anxious to go back to the scene of the find, but he had to show the authorities the location of the body. He was nervous as he and Dick harnessed the team and climbed into the wagon.

Dick drove the team across the south pasture and over the levee to the river's edge, a distance of about three city blocks. Clyde jumped out and stood next to Dad. As soon as he answered the necessary questions, Clyde hurried back to the house on foot, anxious to forget his ghastly find. He didn't wait for a ride back in the wagon, because he knew who the third passenger would be.

Dressed in rubberized pants and coat provided by the sheriff, Todd waded into the water and slipped loops of rope over the body and helped drag it to shore. Then he and the men who came with the sheriff shoved the decomposed corpse into a canvas body bag. Finally they laid the bag in the back of the spring wagon and stuffed their own rainwear into another bag. A putrid stench permeated the air.

"Dick, go ahead and drive back to the house. We'll be there in a few minutes," Dad ordered. "You'd better drive along at a pretty good clip so you can get away from this smell, but don't drive too fast — you don't want to lose your cargo."

Dick took special pride in driving the team hitched to the spring wagon. He had been glad when Clyde walked on back to the house, knowing that he would be the one to drive back. But he hadn't counted on the "passenger" in the canvas bag adding such a new dimension to the trip.

The slightly anxious boy maneuvered the team through the mud as the wagon creaked its way along the river's edge and up to the top of the levee. He gave a timid glance back at his passenger. The bag was still in place.

The downhill side of the levee seemed miles long as the possibility of the body bag sliding forward and lodging under the seat crossed the young driver's mind.

Level ground felt good. Dad was right. Dick was driving out of the horrible smell. It had made him sick to his stomach and he almost threw up, but now his confidence was returning. Then he smelled it again. That awful sickening smell was coming back. Dick glanced back at the canvas bag. It hadn't been tied securely and a badly decomposed and bony foot protruded from the opening.

Suddenly it didn't matter whether his passenger stayed with him or not. Dick snapped the reins and his team leaped into a full gallop.

June, Bill, Johnnie, and I wanted to meet him in the lot, but Mom made us stay in the yard.

"He's sure driving that team fast," Bill commented. "Dad's not gonna like that."

Dick pulled the team to a quick stop and jumped to the ground. As soon as waiting authorities removed the body, Dick drove the wagon to the horse tank. Mom let Johnnie and Bill go out and help him unhitch the team and scrub out the wagon.

"What was it like, Dick?"

"Were you scared? I don't think I would've been scared," Bill added.

"Naw, I wasn't scared. Nothing to be scared of. The guy was dead, wasn't he? I did feel a little weird when I saw his bony foot sticking out of the sack, but it wasn't nothing."

It took awhile for life to get back to normal after the unsettling experience of that day. Dad's familiar bedtime call "Goodnight, girls; goodnight, boys" felt extra comforting as it floated up the stairs quieting "What if..." whispers. Clyde did find the calf he had been looking for, but it wasn't near the levee; it was at the far end of the south pasture.

We never did learn the identity of the dead man in the river, but we sure learned that we had a brave brother. It was a strong 14 year old who guided the team and wagon that carried the lifeless, canvas-wrapped cargo toward its final resting place. But then Dad knew that, or he never would have asked Dick to take the ride.

Ten years later Dick took a longer ride on a ship to Korea where he fought bravely for two years. Mom and Dad worried even more than I did when Dick rode the bay horse home down the willow-lined, rutted road from old Joe McDole's.

Dick was that kind of fellow. He did his duty and sought no reward. His last "ride" on earth ended in 1987. If there are jobs to do in heaven, the Lord can count on Dick.

Chapter II

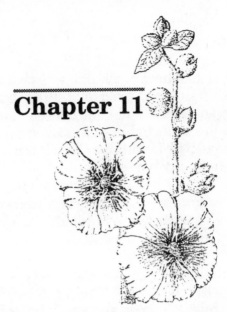

Chapter 11

School's Not Always a "Cinch"

It is from experiences such as mine that we get our education of life.

"Mark Twain, A Biography"

The little one-room, white school house with SMITH SCHOOL DISTRICT #152 painted above the front door housed as many as five little Dunkers at a time. June and Bill's first teacher was Miss Kathryn (Kathryn Distlehorst). She saved Bill's life.

When Bill was in the second grade he sucked instead of blew on a tiny whistle, and it lodged in his throat. The young teacher grabbed the gasping boy by the ankles and flipped him upside down with a jerk. The whistle popped out onto the floor, and Miss Kathryn became a hero at our house. She is to all Dunkers to this day.

When the weather allowed, Dad let the older kids ride the horses to school. "Don't let anyone saddle your horses for you," he warned. "All of you know how to saddle a horse and you'll be safer if you do it yourself."

One day Garnette allowed a classmate to saddle her horse, Old Mike. Laurell had a crush on Garnette. Every day he followed her to where the horse was tied and offered to help her. Finally she got tired of telling him "no." The little seventh grade girl did not return the young man's feelings, but she didn't want to hurt him. Even though she knew Dad would be mad if he found out, she relented. "All right, Laurell, you can saddle my horse."

Dick, John, and Bill were far down the gravel road ahead of Garnette and her second grade passenger, June, by the time Laurell got the horse saddled. The love smitten boy gave Garnette a foot up and lifted June to her place behind the saddle.

"Hang on tight, June," Garnette warned, "I'm gonna try to catch up with the boys." The agile equestrienne gave her horse free rein, and soon she and her passenger were within shouting distance of the boys.

Planting her feet firmly in the stirrups, Garnette leaned forward, encouraging the horse to trot just a little faster. With no warning, the cinch which held the saddle in place pulled loose, freeing the saddle just enough to cause it to slide down onto the horse's side. The sudden, unfamiliar shifting of his load caused Old Mike to rear and buck. "Hang on, June!" Garnette cried frantically.

She looked back in time to see June flying downward to within inches of the sharp hooves of the horse's flailing back feet. A split second later, the saddle slid under the horse's belly with Garnette's foot caught in one stirrup. Dragging Garnette with him, Old Mike danced in a circle in the middle of the path, trying to free the saddle from its belly-side position. Garnette screamed for the boys. They got to the scene in time to see her foot slip free from the stirrup and to see the saddle fall a few feet from the frightened horse.

Dick scooped up a somewhat dazed and frightened June. Johnnie and Bill hurried over to Garnette who was lying in a bruised heap in the middle of the path.

"What in the world happened?" Johnnie asked as he helped the dusty rider to her feet.

"I don't know. The saddle just slipped. Is June all right?" Tears streaked down Garnette's dust covered face.

"She's all right," Dick assured Garnette. "Didn't you saddle your horse yourself?"

"No," Garnette replied wiping tears with the back of her hand. "Laurell did it for me." The toppled rider hid her tear-stained and dust-muddied face in trembling hands.

"You know Dad tells us to always saddle our own horses," Dick reminded her.

"I know," Garnette sobbed even harder. "He's probably really gonna whip me when we get home."

Johnnie and Bill used the calamity to put their "cowboy skills" into action. Heretofore, they had participated only in pretend roundups. Now they were roping a real runaway horse, and they got him. Not wanting to mount the captured animal just yet, the little group walked their horses toward home. "Maybe we won't have to tell Dad," Johnnie offered.

"We'd better," Dick said. "How can we explain Garnette's dirty face and clothes and June's ripped dress?"

"I guess you're right," Garnette agreed, fearing she and Dad's belt would surely meet when she got home.

As the kids trudged slowly through the lot toward the barn, leading their horses behind them, Dad came up, empty feed buckets in hand. "You kids are late tonight. What happened?"

Garnette instinctively knew Dad would be fair, but she feared the worst as she answered him, "My saddle slipped and June and I fell off our horse."

The dreaded question came. "Who in the world saddled your horse, Garnette? You've never had that happen before."

"Well," Garnette began, swallowing a sob, "see, Dad, Laurell wants me to be his girlfriend and he keeps pesterin' me about it all the time and so I let him saddle my horse just to get him to leave me alone for awhile."

June stepped out from behind the boys. Seeing her torn dress, Dad picked her up and began checking her over. "Do you hurt anyplace, June?"

"No, I'm all right. I wasn't scared a bit. Garnette couldn't help it, Dad."

Dad turned to Garnette and said, "You got by lucky this time, Garnette. I hope this teaches you a lesson. From now on, this horse and his saddle are your responsibility when you're at school. If you have any trouble at all, you ask one of the boys."

Relieved, but beginning to feel some aches and pains from her eventful trip home, Garnette walked Old Mike to the barn.

The boys were hanging up saddles and bridles as she entered. "You're lucky," Dick said. If that had been one of us boys, Dad would've probably used the belt on us."

Chapter 12

The Big Lesson

It used to take me all vacation to grow a new hide in place of the one they flogged off me during the school term.

"Mark Twain's Travels with Mr. Brown"

I could hardly wait to start school. It meant learning to read and to write. It meant I would be grown up like June. And, it meant a trip to the Busy Bee Store to get school clothes.

The Busy Bee was in Quincy. The owner stocked bib overalls, work shoes, overshoes, and coats. He also carried girls' dresses, shoes, underwear, and ribbons for my pigtails. We usually made two trips to the Busy Bee Store each year, one in the fall and one in the spring. After we made our selections, Dad would pile them on the counter and make the store owner an offer.

"Tell you what," he'd begin, his hand resting on the stack of much needed clothing, "I've added these things up and the total price comes to seventy-five dollars; I'll give you fifty dollars for the bunch."

"I can't make any money that way, Mr. Dunker." the owner almost always retorted. "Do you think you could give me sixty-five?"

"Fifty-five is it."

"Charlie, if you can give me fifty-seven fifty, you've got a deal."

"You drive a hard bargain," Dad always chortled as he counted out the money, "but since the kids need this stuff, I'll pay the price."

I'm sure that dear store owner made little money from our shopping trips, but he and Dad remained friends throughout the years.

Sometimes Dad made a middle-of-the-winter trip to the Busy Bee which didn't include any of us kids or Mom. It was usually a "shoe trip." Finding us in need of shoes and overshoes, he simply broke sticks the length of our feet and carried them to Quincy. What a treat to come home from school and find a shiny, new pair of shoes which fit perfectly.

Starting to school and getting to go on one of the school shopping Busy Bee trips meant I was growing up. Maybe June and Bill didn't share my excitement about going to school and growing up, but they liked the Busy Bee trip, too.

"School's gonna be a lot of fun," I proclaimed to whoever would listen as we bounced along in the truck.

"I don't think it will," June complained. "We won't have much time to ride horses or chase Slick Blue or any fun stuff. Besides, we're gonna have an old man teacher. I wish Miss Kathryn could come back."

Dad interrupted us. "I don't think you have to worry about your teacher. He seems to be a fairly decent fellow and he and his wife and little boy, Bobby, will be living in a trailer right on the school grounds. His wife will be a helper for him so it will almost be like having two teachers."

"Who needs two teachers to keep us in school when I don't even want one. I can read already, Dad. Why can't I just stay home and help you?" June pleaded. June was going into the third grade which she considered a complete waste of time. She and Bill tagged along with Dad every chance they got, and she couldn't bear being closed inside that schoolhouse while Dad worked alone on the chores she and Bill had helped him with all summer.

"You'll be home in plenty of time to help bring the cows in and even have time to ride your horse before bedtime, June. Maybe this year you'll enjoy school."

"Not with a man teacher I won't," she pouted.

I was worried about the new "man" teacher, too, but I didn't let on. *I wonder if he'll be mean,* I thought, but the pending trip to the Busy Bee soon took over my thoughts and any worry about school was replaced with dreams of what kind of ribbons to buy.

At last school started and the new "man" teacher, Mr. John Druson, didn't seem to be too bad. His wife did come over to the schoolhouse once in awhile and help us with our studies. Her most important job, however, was fixing our lunches. The year 1942 saw rural schools receiving peanut butter and various other commodities for lunches. Mrs. Druson was in charge of the food.

We got along just fine with Mr. Druson through the winter even though, for some unknown reason, he didn't seem to like Bill. With the arrival of spring, we forgot all about Mr. Druson's attitude toward the youngest of the three Dunker boys as the out of doors again beckoned. June and Bill dawdled on the way to school, but were the first ones out the door to go home and dig some worms for fishing.

During this particular spring, my brother-in-law, Dode, made a plywood cover for the back of his pickup truck, put some benches in it and provided the Smith School students with bus service. All the faster for June and Bill to get home.

Mr. Druson had different ideas. "Billie," he said one afternoon just before we left school, "I want you to write ten sentences tonight using the word 'rue' and bring them to school with you in the morning."

"Sure," Bill promised as he ran out the door to catch his ride home. And the word "rue" left Bill's mind until the next morning at school.

After roll call, Mr. Druson asked Bill for the sentences. "Oh, I forgot to do them," came the disinterested reply.

"Well," said Mr. Druson in a most ominous manner, "I

believe you should stay after school tonight and write not only the ten that were due today, but ten more for being late. What do you think, children? Shouldn't Billie have to do his homework like the rest of you?" he asked, addressing the entire room.

A couple of kids agreed with the teacher, but most of us just sat there. It seemed to me like Mr. Druson was asking a lot of Bill, but I wasn't about to disagree with the stern, sometimes almost scary man. That afternoon, Bill stayed in the school house with Mr. Druson while the rest of us filed out the door and onto the bus.

"Where's Billie?" Mom asked as soon as we got home.

"He had to stay after school and write sentences for Mr. Druson," Dick answered her. "He was supposed to do it last night, but we went fishing instead."

"I guess it serves him right," Mom said. "If his teacher told him to do something and he didn't do it, then keeping him after school is the right thing to do."

The rest of us were sitting down to the kitchen table for an after school snack when Johnnie yelled, "Hey, there comes Bill down the lane now. He sure must've got those sentences done in a hurry."

As Bill came into the house, Mom asked, "Did you do the work that Mr. Druson asked you to do?"

"Well, not exactly," Bill answered. "See, Mr. Druson told Mrs. Druson to watch me because he wanted to go fishing, so she came over to the schoolhouse and brought Bobby. They sat there and watched me for just a minute or two, and then Mrs. Druson told me to go on home and finish my work there. So here I am. I ran almost all the way home."

"How many more sentences do you have to write," Mom asked.

"Nineteen. I already wrote one. Rue is a hard word. I thought maybe Garnette would help me tonight."

The evening got away from Bill, and no sentences were written. The next morning, again right after roll call, Mr. Druson asked Bill for his sentences.

"I don't have them," my nine-year old brother told him in

a rather frightened voice. "See I don't know for sure what 'rue' means, so I don't know how to make sentences with it."

"That's no excuse, Billie," Mr. Druson said. He looked so stern that I was becoming frightened. "Just for that, I am going to add ten more sentences, and you can stay after school today and write them."

Off we went that afternoon, leaving Bill in the school house. And no sooner did we get home than we looked back and saw the reluctant student coming up the lane.

When asked about his homework, Bill gave the same answer, "Mr. Druson had Mrs. Druson and Bobby come over so he could go fishing and just as soon as he left, she let me come home."

"You'd better get that work done tonight, Billie," Mom warned. "Get one of the older kids to help you."

Bill didn't tell Mom that he didn't understand the word nor did he ask for help in writing the sentences. Consequently, the next day at school arrived with no sentences to turn in to Mr. Druson.

Mr. Druson didn't ask for sentences after roll call. Instead, he slowly and deliberately pushed his desk against the stage in back of him. Then he slid the recitation bench against the south wall. In an almost sinister stride, he walked over to the tall north windows and removed a four foot stick, about the thickness of a broom handle, from the sill.

"Children," he began in an ominous voice, "Mrs. Druson informs me that Billie has not been writing his sentences after school each night. She tells me that he is leaving early before his work is completed. For this, Billie must be punished."

I don't know that I had ever heard the word "punished" before. To this day my stomach quivers when I hear it.

Mr. Druson sort of slithered down the aisle between the rows of desks. Stopping beside Bill, he reached down and clutched my brother's upper arm, dragging him back to the space created by moving the desk and recitation bench. "This is how we punish little boys who don't do the work assigned by their teacher," he said and he began to hit Bill with the stick.

I started shaking. I was too scared to cry.

Whack! Bill tried desperately to pull away. Mr. Druson's grip slipped from the hurting boy's upper arm and slid down to his small wrist. Whack!

Each time the cruel teacher struck him, Bill lunged forward, trying to free himself from the grasp of his captor's outstretched hand. Mr. Druson dug in his heels and hung on. The resulting scene was a bizarre, circular dance executed by a small, frightened boy and a tall, angular and angry man.

With methodical and, by now, predictable strokes, the unrelenting Mr. Druson continued his punishment. Whack! Whack! Whack!

"Unhh," Bill moaned. He didn't cry. He just turned white. Whack!

"Unhh."

Tears finally gushed down my cheeks. Mr. Druson kept beating Bill — whack! whomp! — not stopping the punishment until the stick broke. Throwing down the broken piece, the angry beast of a man shoved the bruised and frightened child back down the aisle and into his seat. "Now, maybe in the future you'll do your homework," he said in an odd, quiet way. Then, turning directly toward me he ordered, "There's no reason for anyone to be upset. This is merely an example of what happens when children disobey their teacher. Let's get on with our lessons. Patsie Dunker, you can stop crying now."

I felt sick at my stomach. I wanted to run home. The kid behind me whispered, "What's that water running off your seat, Patsie?" He began to giggle.

I looked down. To my horror I discovered I had wet my pants, and a telltale drip, plopping quietly onto the wood floor, was informing the entire room. Somehow we survived the day. When Dick, Johnnie, Bill, June, and I finally got home, we all began to call, "Mom, Mom, where are you? Bill got a whippin'! Bill got a whippin'!"

"I was really scared, Mom," I said. I tugged at her apron in an effort to divert her attention toward me and my embarrassment and discomfort. "I even wet my pants," I whispered to her.

"Just a minute, Patsie; I'll talk to you in just a minute. Quiet down, kids," Mom urged, turning to Johnnie on whom she could always depend for rationality. "Johnnie, what happened at school today?"

"Well, Bill was supposed to write all those sentences for Mr. Druson and didn't get them done, so Mr. Druson whipped him."

Johnnie's statement was true all right, but he didn't say how scared we all were and how Mr. Druson acted as if he was enjoying what he was doing. He didn't even tell Mom that the stick broke and that some of us cried.

Boy, I thought, *I wish Mom had asked me what happened. I could have told her more than Johnnie did. Oh, well, Mom and Dad always say that the teacher knows best so maybe Johnnie told Mom enough.* But I still felt scared and confused.

Mom's voice interrupted my thoughts, "Your dad is gone right now and won't be home until late tonight. I'll have to talk to him about this. All of you change out of your school clothes, and then you boys bring the cows up to the barn."

Turning to me, she asked, "Now, Patsie, what is it you wanted to tell me?"

"Nothing, Mom. Johnnie told you everything. I'd better go change my clothes." I ran off with the rest of the kids, but I was confused about the whole issue.

Later that evening I heard Mom telling Dad that Mr. Druson had whipped Billie. "What did he do to deserve it?" Dad asked.

"He never did write those darned sentences."

"I guess he deserved the whipping then."

Clyde didn't know anything about the events of the day. He had spent most of the afternoon away from home. He came back late that night and discovered Bill's plight as he was readying for bed. Clyde raced downstairs and into Mom and Dad's bedroom. "When I lit the lamp in our room, I saw bruises and welts on Bill from his shoulders to the bend of his knees! What in the world is goin' on?" he shouted.

Dad and Mom ran upstairs with Clyde. The bruised child was sleeping soundly on his stomach. The dim light of the kerosene lamp was enough to enable Mom and Dad to see that the stripes had turned a deep and disturbing blue.

Dad turned to Clyde. "You stay here with your mother and the kids," he ordered.

"What're you gonna do, Dad?"

"I don't know yet, Clyde, but no man should be allowed to hit any little kid the way that man beat Bill."

Clyde was angry with Mr. Druson, too. He wanted to go with Dad, but he knew better than to argue.

Dad drove to Todd's and got him out of bed. "Come go with me to John Druson's trailer. I've got something to settle with him as a parent and a member of the School Board."

"What's happened, Dad? Don't you think we should let whatever it is settle 'til tomorrow?" Todd asked, pulling on his clothes.

"No, I don't. He nearly beat Bill to death. I'm gonna see him tonight."

"What do you mean 'beat him?' Is Bill hurt?"

"I'll tell you about it on the way. Let's go."

Dad described Bill's bruises to Todd as they drove to the teacher's trailer. When Dad's truck pulled up beside Mr. Druson's home, Todd had heard enough. The protective big brother jumped out of the nearly stopped vehicle and began pounding on the trailer door. "Druson, John Druson," he demanded, "Get out here and tell us your side of the story about Bill's so called 'spanking.'"

"I don't know what you're talking about," Mr. Druson whined from behind the closed trailer door.

"Open your door and I'll tell you what I'm talking about," Todd ordered. Mr. Druson cautiously opened the door. Todd pulled him out onto the steps and gave him a swift poke in the jaw. In his attempt to get away from Todd, poor Mr. Druson stumbled into Dad who gave him a boot in the rear.

"You start packing. And don't show up for school tomorrow!" Dad ordered. "A normal spanking with a ruler is what most teachers give their students. I've never heard of a beating like you gave Bill."

The next day and on into the next two weeks, we didn't have school. Bill was a hero at our house. Mr. Druson left with no explanation to any of the other school board members. During a special board meeting, Dad explained the events that led up to the teacher's departure. Dad's fellow board members agreed that he should have been dismissed — maybe in a slightly different fashion, but nonetheless dismissed.

Miss Kathryn, the teacher who had saved Bill's life, finished out the term. and school became a pleasant experience again, even for June and Bill.

Wilbur, the first in our family to graduate from high school, was in the Air Force when Mr. Druson beat Bill. Mom sent him all the details in a letter. Wilbur wrote back, "Mom, here's a sentence for that teacher: 'John Druson, you'll rue the day that you beat my brother.'"

We never saw Mr. Druson again, except for the time he came down to the annual Hull picnic. The "three boys" let the air out of all four of his truck tires. The next morning at the breakfast table they told Dad what they did. He laughed.

Chapter 13

Miss Mundy Had a Way

Learning softeneth the heart and breedeth gentleness and charity.

"The Prince and the Pauper"

Helen Brinkman Mundy was her name. She replaced the infamous Mr. Druson. We called her "Miss" Mundy. She had a coal-black terrier dog named "Africa." She gave the little dog that name because her husband, David, was stationed in Africa during the Second World War.

Africa was an occasional visitor at Smith School. He could sing. He couldn't carry a tune, but he barked and howled when Miss Mundy played "Dance With a Dollie With a Hole in Her Stocking" and "Don't Sweetheart Me" on the school piano. Africa didn't know any other songs. He sat silently beside his young mistress while she played "America" for us to sing each morning. No matter what else she played, the little dog would sit closed-mouth beside her, waiting for the familiar bouncy rhythm of his two favorite songs.

Africa could count, too. "Three, Africa," Miss Mundy would say and the little dog would return with "Yip, yip, yip." He could only count to five, but we thought he was awful smart.

Cold weather found Garnette, June, and I wearing long brown cotton stockings to school. They were held up by supporters attached to our trap-door underwear. Each morning we pulled on the hated stockings, and by noon our knees bagged so that we looked like we had a serious skin malady. Mom made us start wearing the dreaded brown addition to our winter wardrobe as soon as the first cold spell arrived. They protected our legs from the cold, but I would learn that they could not protect me from the consequences of my clumsiness.

"Don't run, Patsie," Johnnie had warned on the way home from school, "you're liable to fall in the gravel." I ran. Johnnie was right. I fell on my knees in the sharp-edged gravel.

"Oh-h-h," I wailed, "I hurt my knees. Help me."

Dick, Johnnie, Bill, and June all raced to my rescue. They stood me in the middle of the road. Together we surveyed the damage. The knees of my long brown stockings were torn and hanging in bloody shreds. When I saw the deep cuts, I cried louder. "They hurt! They hurt! I can't walk."

Dick lifted me tenderly to his shoulders and carried me home. June and Bill beat a hasty path to the house to warn Mom of her coming patient.

After Mom washed my mangled knees with boiled water and soap, she wrapped them with strips of an old sheet smeared with Rawleigh's Black Salve. Then she put clean, long brown stockings over the bandages. My knees looked like I had a soft ball stuffed in each stocking.

"I don't want to wear them, Mom, please. They look awful."

Mom lifted me down from the table. "Now, listen, young lady, if it hadn't been for those stockings, your legs would look a lot worse than they do now."

I wore long brown stockings the rest of the winter. Today, I have a one inch scar on each knee. Mom was probably right; the scars could be two inches long.

Our school house was heated with a big, tin-jacketed coal stove which stood in the northwest corner of the building. Miss Mundy had to fire the stove each morning. We had to wear extra warm clothes during the cold months, because sometimes our contrary heating system wouldn't warm the room much before noon. Severe cold weather would find the entire student body of Smith School huddled together on a long wooden bench beside the stove.

Two or three times a winter, the temperamental contraption belched puffs of smoke from around it's heavy and tightly latched door. Miss Mundy opened some of the tall north windows to clear the room of the acrid smoke. I wouldn't admit it to Mom, but those brown stockings felt pretty good on days like that.

Miss Mundy loved music. Each year Smith School, under her expert direction, produced and performed three programs: one in the fall, one at Christmastime, and one in the spring. Our multi-talented teacher provided the piano accompaniment.

Over the years, the velvet-curtain-flanked stage had held a variety of tongue-tied performers. All too often, upon arriving center stage, a well rehearsed "piece" could not be called to mind. While I had little trouble saying my piece, I would join the ranks of the speechless. I had volunteered to sing.

I learned the song, "Put Your Arms Around Me, Honey." Since speaking was almost fun for me, I just knew that I could sing a song. We sang all the time at home, and I could carry a tune quite well, so I didn't worry about my singing debut.

Gas lamps, hanging from hooks on the ceiling, lighted the little school room, creating a warm, pleasant atmosphere as proud parents and excited students gathered for the evening of entertainment. "Patsie," Miss Mundy coached, "when you sing the first line 'Put your arms around me, Honey,' hug yourself with both arms for just a minute. And when you sing 'Oh, oh, won't you roll those eyes,' you might roll your eyes just a time or two."

Armed with these well intended suggestions, I walked out onto the stage. A quavering, little voice, hardly discernible beyond the first row of the audience, was all that I could offer. Fear gripped my very being. Per my teacher's instructions, I wrapped myself in a tight hug and rolled my eyes toward the ceiling. But she hadn't intended for me to sing the entire song frozen in that contorted position.

At the song's end, I curtsyed to polite applause and ran from the stage. Miss Mundy smiled at me, but I knew how badly I had done. I gave serious consideration to running away and never coming back to school.

However, the following Monday I awoke with the realization that there is life after "the stage" and walked to school with the rest of the kids. But I have often wondered if dear Miss Mundy suggested to my classmates that there would be no discussion of the previous Friday's program. Nobody said a word to me about my debut.

Nobody, that is, except Nancy, Pearl's daughter and my first-grader niece.

"Boy, you sure can roll your eyes," she affirmed.

Smith School had a band. It had a wind section and a percussion section. The wind section boasted a water whistle and numerous kazoos. I was a percussionist. I played the sand blocks. Johnnie played the sticks. We also had some tambourines and a jingly thing on the end of a stick. I don't know what it was called.

We even had uniforms for our Smith School Rhythm Band. Our mothers made red and white capes and covered oatmeal boxes with colored paper. We wore the boxes for hats. We even took our band on the road. We played for the brave people in Miss Mundy's church.

One day, after we pledged the flag, sang "God Bless America," and listened to a Bible story, Miss Mundy made an announcement: "Children, today we are going to start reading the story of Tom Sawyer. This story was written by a man named Samuel Langhorne Clemens, but he signed his stories with the name Mark Twain. When he was a boy, Samuel Clemens lived just across the river from our schoolhouse. He lived in Hannibal, Missouri."

Bill raised his hand. "You know what, Miss Mundy? Sometimes when me and Johnnie and Dick are over at one of the islands in the river by our house, we can hear sounds from Hannibal." Miss Mundy smiled at Bill. She had a way of making us feel so important.

During the ensuing weeks we became acquainted with Tom Sawyer and Aunt Polly, and we learned why Samuel Clemens took the name of Mark Twain. Once or twice I lost track of the story and gave full attention to the portraits of George Washington, Blue Boy, and Pink Lady which hung on the south wall of our school.

A large Regulator Clock shared the wall with the famous paintings. Its rhythmic, soft counting of the hours could lull a first grader to sleep once in awhile. But Tom Sawyer's story won out, and Becky Thatcher became a heroine of mine. I figured any girl who could stay in a cave without a light had to be made of strong stuff. And I wondered if Huckleberry Finn really did smoke a pipe. "Dad sure would get on the three boys if he ever caught them smoking a pipe," I mused.

When she reached the end of the book, Miss Mundy said, "I have a surprise for you. I have made arrangements for all of us to catch the train that stops in Hull and ride in it all the way to Hannibal. We are going to visit Mark Twain's home, and then go to the cave where Tom and Becky got lost."

The home and cave were interesting, but the museum fascinated me. A pilot's wheel from a riverboat, anchored to a post in the floor, stood within easy reach of museum visitors. I turned it. I tried to imagine what it would be like if the wheel was attached to its original riverboat and I was steering it down the river past our house. *I would blow the whistle to let Mom know I where I was,* I thought.

Dad picked up five tired kids at the little train station in Hull at the end of our day. That night I dreamed that I saw Injun Joe and that I had been trapped in the cave with Becky Thatcher. I wasn't as brave as she had been.

In retrospect, I know that Mrs. Helen Brinkman Mundy was a true teacher. She was blessed with the ability to instill in us an excitement about learning. A short time ago, I took a college literature course. The required reading list included Huckleberry Finn.

I read of how Huckleberry ran away from his pap and floated to an island on the Illinois side of the river. The free-spirited adventurer noted that he could hear the sounds

of Hannibal as he lay in the bottom of a canoe. Something
stirred in my memory —

"You know what, Miss Mundy? ...me and Johnnie and
Dick...can hear sounds from Hannibal."

Chapter 14

"Clyder, Sweet as Apple Cider"

It is not best that we should all think alike; it is dif-
ferences of opinion that makes horse races.

"Pudd'nhead Wilson's Calendar"

On May 30, 1925, when they carried almost three-year-old
Wilbur into Mom's bedroom to get a first glimpse of his tiny
blue-eyed baby brother, he said, "Oh, no, Mom. Why did you
get him?" But this little boy couldn't know what kind of
brother Clyde would be. Nobody on that day could know of
the joy and the profound love for life that Clyde would teach
us all.

The circumstances of Christmas that year of 1925 befit the
way Clyde would live his life. At first the holiday season
looked as though it would be bleak. After settling his debts,
Dad had only a ten dollar bill to spend on gifts for his seven
children, Mom, and Grandma Dunker who was visiting.

He stood by the kitchen window rubbing the bill between
his thumb and fingers. "Sure can't get much of a Christmas
for the kids and you and my maw with this," he worried.

"Charlie, don't concern yourself so. I don't need anything.
We can get a little something for the kids and your mother

with that money. I know we can't get much, but the kids will enjoy whatever they get. You can't help the way prices have been."

Mom had told Dad earlier she needed to get a few yards of material so she could make a couple of house dresses for herself. He felt bad that he didn't have enough extra money for her to buy even enough yard goods for one dress. He knew that she wouldn't spend any of the ten dollars on herself without getting Christmas presents for the kids first.

"Come on, Charlie, breakfast is ready. These pancakes will get cold. Why don't you try to forget about it. We'll figure something out. We always do."

Dad remained by the window, absentmindedly rubbing the bill between his thumb and fingers.

"Corrie! Look! I have two, brand new ten dollar bills." Dad waved them in the air.

"Where did they come from? How did you get two?" Mom couldn't believe what she was seeing.

"I don't know how it happened, but when I was rubbing this one it split, and now I have two." Mom's surprise and disbelief changed to joy and relief.

"Get your coat, Corrie. Maw will stay here with the kids; we have some Christmas shopping to do!" Dad called to her as he raced outside to start the old car.

If Clyde had been old enough to have been cognizant of the little Christmas miracle, he would have loved it; he loved happy endings.

Clyde, who was eleven years older than me, was my big buddy. I called him "Clyder, Sweet as Apple Cider" and he called me "Jimmer." I don't know why Clyde called me Jimmer, but he did. Clyde did things like that. Often he sang "Tiny Turned Up Nose" to me and carried me around on his shoulders.

One night when June and I were taking turns riding on his shoulders, I got the giggles and did a terrible thing.

"Mom, come get this kid," he yelled, "she wet down my neck!"

But I know he forgave me because that was the winter

Mary Ellen arrived. I was four and a half years old that Christmas, but the memory of the first time I saw that doll stays bright in my heart.

Fifteen-year-old Clyde trapped muskrat and mink during the winter and sold the pelts for spending money. Like everyone in our family, he shared part of his earnings with the rest of us. A few days before Christmas, this wonderful brother of mine rode up to Quincy with Dad.

They got home just as we were sitting down at the dinner table. "Jimmer," Clyde began with a twinkle in his eye that matched the holiday season, "I saw the darndest thing in Quincy today. I saw a ragged old dollie. Her dress was torn and she only had one shoe, but I felt so sorry for her that I bought her anyway."

My little girl heart went out to the bedraggled doll even before I saw her. I pictured a homely, streaked-face baby badly in need of my attention. I turned to Mom. "Mom, do you think we can make her some clothes?"

"Oh, I've already checked with Santy, Jimmer," Clyde assured. "He said that he'd do the best he could with her, but he wouldn't make any promises." Clyde hung his winter hat in the closet and tried with his usual lack of success to smooth his curly brown hair, his face wreathed in smiles and excitement. He sat down in his chair at the end of the dinner table. "Santy said he'd bring the doll sometime around Christmas."

Being accustomed to hand-me-down clothes and few toys, I thought the arrival of a second-hand doll would be nice. So I waited. Clyde mentioned the doll every little bit those few days before Christmas.

"Sure is a homely old thing, Jimmer," he would say, "but I know you'll love her." Then he would give me a goodnight hug and go on his way.

On Christmas Eve, just before Garnette, Dick, Johnnie, Bill, June, and I hid in the kitchen closet so that Santa could stomp across the kitchen floor, Clyde slipped over and whispered to me, "Now, Jimmer, don't feel too bad about the dollie. I know Santy did his best."

I wasn't worried. If Santa had trouble making her pretty,

I knew Mom would fix her. Mom could fix anything. I hid in the closet with the rest of the kids.

"Ho, ho, ho!" Santa was walking across our kitchen and heading for our Christmas tree! I quivered with anticipation. Finally, Clyde threw open the closet door and we scrambled into the living room.

Leaning against our paper-chain decorated cedar Christmas tree, with the warm light of the kerosene lamp dancing in her eyes, sat Mary Ellen. She was everything any little girl could ever dream of in a doll. She wasn't made-over; she was brand spanking new.

The beautiful big baby doll with the "real sleeping eyes" was wearing a fur-trimmed, pink wool coat and matching bonnet. Delicate little anklets topped with soft white leather shoes covered her fat feet. The full skirt of a pink organdy dress forced its way from beneath the folds of the coat and a flower-embroidered slip with matching underpanties completed her wardrobe.

"Looks like Santy did a pretty good job, didn't he Patsie Ellen?"

Clyde would drop my nickname when he was filled with emotion or when he had to be serious with me about something. That night I think he was filled with the emotion that only the love and wonder of Christmas brings. I know I was.

I remember another time when Clyde dropped my nickname, only this time he was serious, very serious.

Mom hadn't been feeling well that spring of 1944. Pearl came down now and then to help out or to take two or three of us home with her for an afternoon. But nothing worked. Mom didn't get any better.

Late one night during mid-April Dad called up the stairs, "Clyde, you and Garnette come down here." All of us heard him, but only Garnette and Clyde raced down the stairs. The rest of us knew not to go unless we had been asked.

Indiscernible muffled sounds floated up to our bedrooms. Once or twice we thought we heard moans. "You kids do whatever Garnette and Clyde say; I have to leave for a little bit." The tone of Dad's voice was unmistakable. It told us that trouble was afoot. We heard the old blue Hudson leave the lot.

It seemed like hours before Clyde came up the stairs. June and I were sitting up in bed when he brought the three boys into our room. "What's wrong, Clyde?" June's face, lighted by Garnette's little brown kerosene lamp which Clyde held in his hand, betrayed her attempt to appear calm.

"Now, I don't want you kids to be scared, but you have to be real, real quiet and real, real good. Mom's awful sick. Dad went up to Pearl's to call the doctor."

I started to cry. "I'm scared, Clyde," I sniffed.

"Now, Patsie Ellen, you can't cry. We don't want to worry Mom."

Downstairs, Garnette was standing beside our mother's bed. The fifteen year old dutifully mopped the brow of her deathly white and sick patient. "Mom, Mom," the frightened girl cried, "are you alive?" No answer came to relieve Garnette's rising panic. Briskly she rubbed Mom's arms and slapped her silent face.

"Oh-h-h." Relief washed over Garnette when she heard Mom's low moan.

Dad's car came flying up our lane. Pearl's husband, Karl, was with him. Dad carried Mom to the waiting car and Karl drove them to the hospital in Hannibal. It was agreed that Pearl would stay near her phone so that news of Mom's condition could be received and brought to us.

Midmorning of the next day, Dad called Pearl, and she hurried down to tell us the news of Mom. "Here she comes; here she comes," Garnette called to us. "Now we'll find out how Mom is."

"Mom's fine, kids," Pearl assured the frightened group of siblings who met her at the door. "She had a very bad gall bladder attack and she had an operation this morning. She'll be in the hospital for quite awhile, but she's going to be just fine."

"Kids," Clyde ordered, "we're gonna have to be extra good when Mom gets home. She'll be weak for quite awhile. Boys, don't be starting any fights and girls, you're gonna have to help Garnette while Mom's gone and for a long time after she gets home."

We made it through two long weeks, and then Mom came home. Even though I was almost eight, I still sat on her lap now and then. She would rock me and we would sing "Comin' in on a Wing and a Prayer." Singing the song made us feel close to Wilbur while he was in the Air Force. But it made us cry, too.

Anyway, the first thing the three boys and June said to me when Mom walked slowly through the door into the living room was, "You can't sit on Mom's lap anymore. You'll hurt her incision, won't she, Dad?"

Dad was helping Mom ease down into our favorite rocking chair. "I guess that'll have to be up to your mother," he answered.

I stood forlornly in the doorway while the rest of the kids were getting and giving hugs and kisses. Sensing my uneasiness, Mom beckoned to me. "Come here, Patsie Ellen, and give me a kiss."

I sure had missed that smile. Even though I longed to climb up in her lap, I just walked slowly toward her and stood beside the chair.

"Come on, Sweetheart," her gentle voice urged, "and give me a hug and a kiss. You aren't going to hurt me."

It seemed forever before I got to sit on Mom's lap again. When I did, the other kids teased, "Hey, you're sitting on the wrong side. You're gonna hurt Mom's incision."

If Clyde was in the house when they teased he would say, "She's not hurting Mom. You kids had better quit teasing Patsie." Then turning to Mom, he would whisper to her, "She's not hurting you, is she, Mom?"

Mom always smiled that wonderful sweet smile and answered, "No, Clyde, she's not hurting me."

On June 19, 1944, just a couple of months after Mom's surgery, eighteen-year-old Clyde married Helen Brown and left our home.

Dad got drunk.

Early that morning Dad had repeated for the hundredth

time, "Clyde, you're too young to get married. You'd better wait a couple of years until you can get ahead a little bit."

"Dad, we're gonna be fine. I can make enough money to support us." Clyde didn't want to argue anymore with Dad about getting married. The two had exchanged enough angry words.

After Wilbur had joined the Air Force, Clyde was Dad's only help around the farm. Dick, Johnnie, and Bill were helpers, but too young to shoulder the responsibilities of planting and harvesting. I guess the government understood this kind of predicament, because a rule was implemented which exempted one son of military age from the armed service. And Clyde was that son at our house. He fought the war by plowing the fields and harvesting the crops — by caring for livestock and improving the land. Clyde took his position as Dad's right hand very seriously. He worked hard and often gave Dad some workable, new ideas. Clyde loved this farm and knew, too, that he would work just as hard after he was married.

Dad and Clyde were standing on the north kitchen porch talking about the pending marriage when I stepped out on my way to the wash house to feed my kittens. "Good morning, Clyde. Now that you're eighteen and a grown up man and you're gonna get married, you can be your own boss, can't you?"

"I hope so, Patsie Ellen, I hope so." A sad Clyde, a Clyde I rarely saw turned and entered the kitchen, leaving Dad standing on the porch staring out across the slough.

"What do you want, Patsie?" Dad asked. He was almost hateful.

"Nothing. I'm just gonna go feed the cats." Dad sort of looked through me and then turned and continued staring across the slough and out over the pasture to the little three-room house at the end of the lane that we called "the cottage." Helen and Clyde had been fixing it up to live in after they were married.

Clyde busied himself that morning by taking his clothes and other belongings down the lane to the cottage. Dad was short tempered and strangely silent.

Right after our noon meal, Dad said to Mom, "I'm gonna run in town for awhile; I don't know for sure when I'll be home."

"Remember, Clyde wants to borrow the Hudson tonight. You know that he and Helen are to be in Kinderhook at seven o'clock this evening to get married."

Dad just looked at Mom and left.

Dad and Clyde were two of a kind. They were creative; they loved horses; they were horse traders. They weren't "horse traders" with a negative connotation; they were tradesmen whose first consideration was to make a good and fair deal.

As farmers, they were unrivaled. Dad seemed to know just when to plant and just what to plant. He noted with great pride that his own strong sense of farming was quite evident in the young man who would soon be leaving our household. Dad didn't want him to leave, not just yet.

It's not that Dad didn't like Helen. He did. But he could see so much ahead for the young, single Clyde. The depression was over. Dad could see a chance for this son to get ahead in farming before he brought a wife and one day a family into his life. Clyde didn't see it that way.

Maybe that's why Dad got drunk that day. Or maybe it was because still another child was leaving the nest.

A little after nine o'clock that night, Clyde and Mom were seated at the kitchen table. "He knew I needed the car, didn't he, Mom? He knew I was supposed to pick Helen up at seven, didn't he?"

"Yes, Clyde, he did."

"Well, where is he then?" Clyde left the table and walked over to the window. The headlights of the old, blue Hudson could be seen weaving down our lane. The car pulled into the lot and stopped short of its usual parking spot.

Clyde ran outside and met Dad staggering toward the house. "I'm still gonna marry her tonight, Dad," he cried and jumped into the car. Dad didn't turn to watch the car speed down the lane. A slow and unsteady step brought my slump-shouldered father toward the house.

Mom didn't ask Dad where he had been. She made no accusations. She understood.

There'll never be another Clyder, Sweet as Apple Cider. He entered this world on a holiday and left it on a holiday. He was the first of the 13 Dunker kids to leave the fold, and I'm sure Heaven hasn't been the same since.

Chapter 15

"The Change in Dad's Pocket"

...but the wise man saith, "Put all your eggs in the one basket and — WATCH THAT BASKET."

"Pudd'nhead Wilson"

During the spring of 1945, Gabriel Heatter was indeed announcing "...good news tonight." The Second World War had ended and Wilbur would be coming home. But I wasn't all that happy. Oh, I was happy because Wilbur would be home, but his homecoming was also part of my worry. Mom found me sitting on the bottom step of the stairway, crying.

"What's the matter, Patsie? Are you sick?"

"No, I'm worried about Wilbur."

"You don't need to; he's coming home." Mom smiled and dried my tears with the tail of her apron.

"Yes, but he won't know where to come to. Why do we have to move, Mom? I like it here; it's my home. Does Wilbur know where the new farm is? Will he know how to get to his new home?"

"Yes, he'll know," Mom assured me.

"Yes, but maybe he won't. What if you lose him again? You know you told me you left him in Mason City that time when

he was a little boy and Dick was a baby. He didn't know how
to get home then. Dad had to go get him."

"Well, we won't lose him this time. Don't you worry."

Remembering that Dad had gone back to town for his lost
son eased my concern. I decided that if Wilbur couldn't find
us, Dad would find him and return him to us, but I still
couldn't understand why Dad wanted to move.

Dad had built a rose house shortly after moving his family
to Pike County. He wove sapling willows into a Quonset
shaped frame. Shoots from Mom's pink climbing rose, which
graced the south porch found themselves transplanted
around the base of the willow frame.

By the time I turned six, the little four-by-six foot rose
house, standing five feet high and covered with waxy green
leaves and soft pink blossoms, was firmly established near
the southeast corner of the yard. I loved it. When June was
not riding horseback with the three boys or helping Dad do
chores, she played in the rose house with me. Mainly, though,
Mary Ellen and I set up housekeeping there.

One spring morning Dad had called June and me to the
kitchen window. "Look, do you see the thrush at the door of
the rose house? She has a nest in there. You girls will have
to stay out until her eggs hatch." That's the way Dad was. He
knew every bird and wild animal haunt on our whole farm,
and he respected their needs. He didn't know anything about
that new place.

Why would he want to leave the little rose house or the lily
pond he and Ruby had built under the giant cottonwood and
maple trees in the southwest corner of the yard? And the
sapling willow seats they wove around the big trees — I just
knew there could never be another place like that in the
whole world.

A real worry for me was the new school I would be attending. I hated the thought of going to a "town school." I didn't
know many of the girls in Hull, but the ones I knew seemed
so much more sophisticated and worldly wise than I could
ever be. I was a shy, green, little country kid. How would I
ever get acquainted with all those new kids in town?

"Patsie, your Dad's going into Hull. Would you like to ride along?" No doubt Mom was tired of my long face.

I climbed into the truck with Dad. "I have to get your mother some flour and sugar and toilet soap. Here, take my pencil and write those things down on this piece of paper." Dad removed his indelible pencil, with the half-bullet shaped cap, from its slot in the bib of his overalls. Then he tore a piece from the little note book he always carried. Dad was a hip pocket farmer. He kept a record of all business transactions in the little notebook, hanging bills of sale, etc., on a wire hook in the kitchen.

Carefully I wrote the words "flour" and "sugar" on the note paper. I didn't know for sure how to spell "toilet soap" (I thought it was one long word) so I left it off the note. Then I handed the pencil back to Dad. Woe to the kid who borrowed that pencil and didn't return it.

I tagged after Dad while he ran his errands. Our last stop was Mr. McBride's grocery store. I liked going in there. Mr. McBride was a white-haired round little man who always wore a white shirt and a white apron.

"Good afternoon, Charlie," the pleasant little proprietor greeted us. "Hear you're moving to a new place just outside Hull." Turning to me, he continued, "I'll bet you're looking forward to coming to a new school, Patsie."

I was standing as close to Dad's legs as I could without getting stepped on. Timidly I looked up at Mr. McBride and muttered, "Uh, huh."

"What can I do for you today, Charlie?" the grocer asked.

"The wife wants twenty-five pounds of flour and ten pounds of sugar and... hm-m-m, I thought she wanted something else. What else did she ask us to get, Patsie? Check your list and see if I'm forgetting something."

I just stood there and stared at my shoes. "Nothing."

"That's funny," Dad began again, "I could've swore she wanted three things. Well, I guess not. That'll be it, Mac," he said to Mr. McBride as he paid for the sugar and flour.

On the way home, we drove by our new home. "There it is, Patsie; there's where you'll be living in a few more weeks."

I looked out the window at the big, two story, white house. "It doesn't have any screened-in porches," I complained. "And if you get Mom a new gas stove for the kitchen, where will we put the baby spring lambs?"

Dad laughed. "We'll figure something out. It has electricity and running water and as soon as we get moved, we're going to build a bathroom."

Dad's mention of a bathroom brought the third item on Mom's list to my mind — toilet soap. I had seen the rows of sweet smelling bath soap, Camay, Lifebuoy, and others, lined high on the grocer's shelves. I knew all along that Mom wanted bath soap or "toilet" soap as she called it, but I could not bring myself to say "toilet" in front of Mr. McBride. I couldn't imagine how in the world I would get along in a town school as bashful as I was.

"Well we'd better get on home," Dad said. "Your mother's waiting for these groceries."

"Where's the soap?" Mom asked as Dad set the flour and sugar on the table.

"Soap. That was it. Patsie, your mother wanted us to bring soap. I knew she wanted three things."

I burst into tears.

"What's wrong, now?" Mom asked. "Are you sure you're not sick?"

"I can't move to town, Mom. I knew you wanted toilet soap, but I was afraid to say toilet in front of Mr. McBride."

Mom and Dad looked at each other with that "life is good" look which they shared a lot those days. They smiled a lot those days, too, but I certainly couldn't understand why.

I knew they had had electricity and a telephone in some of their former homes, and I knew that they were looking forward to those conveniences again. I, too, was aware of the convenience of electricity, but I could live without it. After all, we had been living without it for nine years; I couldn't see that we had suffered. And I had finally been included in the Slick Blue chases — I didn't want to give that up just to flip a light switch. Just the last time we chased Slick Blue, he jumped out of the haymow and limped out across the east pasture. "He's hurt this time," June said. "I bet we get him next year." I couldn't imagine a summer without a Slick Blue chase.

I didn't care that the house near Hull had running water, either. The pump in our kitchen and the foot tub on the north kitchen porch for rinsing summer-dirty bare feet suited me just fine.

I wandered into the living room and sat down at the piano. Garnette had taught me to play the piano when I was a very little girl. I could pick out simple melodies, so she taught me to put chords with them. Adding this new dimension to my meager musical skills opened new doors for me. Our old piano became my friend. I went to it when I was happy and challenged myself to learn new songs. I went to it when I was sad and played old familiar tunes. Today I was sad, so I chose a sad song. All of a sudden, an awful thought came to me. *What if the living room floor in the new house won't hold the piano?*

The piano had broken through the living room floor when Mom and Dad moved to this house near the river. It didn't fall into the cellar, but it did create a major repair job. Mom had suggested, though not very convincingly, that they should haul it back to Mason City and give it to Aunt Sarah. Dad would hear nothing of it. He and Todd set to work and reinforced the floor so that it would hold the piano.

The piano was special and I knew it. Long before I was born, when the older kids were little, Dad had bought it for his family. A piano salesman had come through the area offering to leave a player piano in any home for one week. If, after the end of that week, the recipients chose not to keep the wondrous source of unlimited music, he would remove the piano — no strings attached.

At the end of their week Mom had said to Dad, "Charlie, that piano salesman will be in town today, so when you go in to settle up for the corn you sold, tell him to come and get the piano. We just can't afford to keep it."

Dad loaded the wagon with corn and drove into Mason City. A couple of hours later, Mom saw him flying down the road

— holding the reins of the galloping team in one hand and waving a player piano roll in the other. She went down to the gate to meet him. "We own a piano, Corrie," he announced as he handed her the piano roll. "I got a better price than I'd expected for the corn, so now we can have music whenever we want it. Here, go put this roll in that piano and let's hear it."

Through the years, the player part of the piano had ceased to operate, but the keys still worked and the tone was still good. Mom taught me to play "Red Wing" on it. Now, I had to worry that we might not move it to the new house, because it might fall through that floor, too. I was afraid that with all the other plans Dad had for the new farm, he wouldn't take the time to fix another floor.

We moved that spring of 1945, to the big white house with the wide open porches on the farm close to Hull. We had running water and electricity and Mom bought ruffled, crisscrossed curtains to hang on the windows in the parlor. Dad bought her a new sofa with a matching chair for that room. For the first time since they had been married, Mom had a very pretty room to sit in when Mason City relatives came to visit. We kids started going to church on a more regular basis.

Wilbur came home from the Air Force right after we moved and married Charlotte Mosley, the fair young daughter of a local farmer. They, too, started housekeeping on a farm.

Clyde and Helen moved to our house by the river, and the business of farming went on.

Good and bad happened in our nation. The war ended, but President Franklin D. Roosevelt died a few weeks before. Mom and Dad mourned his passing.

I couldn't know what buying that farm meant to to Dad, the son of a German immigrant, whose own maw and paw had separated when he was ten. His innate stubborn pride, which had surfaced even at that tender age, wouldn't allow him to go live with his married sister, Sophia and her new husband, our Uncle Steve. And his stubborn pride wouldn't let him stay in the little back room of the local grocery store without paying the elderly couple who owned the store. So he shined shoes. And he made a vow to himself that he would never be without some change in his pocket.

To me, that was just a story of a little boy who lived a long time ago. I couldn't understand what that story had to do with buying a farm.

One day I would realize that it had everything to do with buying a farm. The pride of the little shoe shine boy was evident the day the change in his pocket helped Dad and Mom to buy the farm near Hull.

In all of my memory, I can never recall a time that Dad didn't have some change in his pocket. When any of us kids asked for a nickel or two, he would dig into that righthand pocket and bring out a handful of change. "Here," he would say, "pick out your nickel."

He did this for his grandchildren too. Grandchildren were very special to Mom and Dad.

As each grandchild arrived, Mom would proclaim, "This is the prettiest one yet, Charlie, don't you think so?"

Dad would laugh, "Oh, Corrie, you always say that."

There came a time when glaucoma took Dad's sight completely. Then Mom would lay a new grandchild in his arms and say, "Look at this one Charlie, it's the prettiest one yet."

Gentle fingertips worked their way softly across each tiny baby's face as he became acquainted with the newest Dunker.

When I placed my first born in his gentle, work-worn hands, he tenderly caressed her face and smiled. "She has your mouth, Pat. She's a pretty baby."

While Dad "saw" both of my daughters, every now and then when I look at my son, I feel an ache in my heart. Tom is the only grandchild never to have known his grandparent's touch.

During the lingering illness that took Dad from us, his trousers hung on a hook in his bedroom closet waiting for him to slip back into them. It was not meant to be. Dad left us on January 16, 1969, at the age of 77. When his trousers were removed from that hook for the last time, a handful of change jingled in the righthand pocket.

I can never forget the house near the Mississippi River where I spent my gentle, little girl years. A few days ago, I drove down to that farm. It has changed. The sloughs are gone, and the pastures which held our cows and sheep have been tilled and planted in grain. Due to government regulations, the river levee has been restructured. It is much broader than it was when I played in its burr-filled sand. All of the trees between the house and the levee have been dozed out. The result is an economically efficient, grain producing farm with a padlocked gate at the end of the lane.

The barn with the gambrel roof, the new barn, and the corn crib where I sang "Mexicali Rose" to Peachy Thomas, are all gone. They have been replaced with a large, maintenance-free metal machine shed.

Spindly hollyhocks still grow in the fence row, but the woven-wire fence no longer encompasses a lush green yard. Weeds and wild vines cover the lily pond. The willow seats Dad made, which so gracefully encircled the cottonwoods, have disappeared.

The old house so dear to my family is empty. The rooms which seemed so large and held so many people are small; their windows have a broken pane here and there. The kitchen, where our big dinner table and cookstove stood, and the living room, where we sat listening to war news on the battery operated radio, were not the spacious sanctuaries of my youth. I couldn't imagine ever having been comfortable in those tiny rooms.

I walked out into the front yard. My thoughts drifted. I saw blond-headed kids and dogs and kittens. The kitchen porch held Mom, calling us in to dinner. Bill and June were riding in on their horses and a little pigtailed girl with a big doll in her arms was coming out of the rose house. Dad was washing up at the outside pump. The hollyhocks were in full bloom.

The great sycamore tree which held my swing stirred in the breeze.

"Well, at least the sycamore is still here. This sure was a pretty place when we were kids, wasn't it, Pat?" Garnette stood next to me.

"Yes," I agreed, "it was a pretty place."

When I returned to my home near Barry, I called Dick Kramer, who oversees the farm. "Dick, I put the gate key back," I informed him. Then I gathered the courage to ask, "When are you going to tear the place down?"

"Maybe in three or four months. I don't know for sure. I do know that it needs to go, though. It's served its purpose. It's worn out."

Dick Kramer's words hit hard. I knew he was right, but I didn't want to see it happen. "You know, Dick, it's hard for me to speak of the house so objectively and to know that it's going to be torn down. It was my home — a place filled with life and love. Now, we are calling it a worn out building."

"But Pat, even when the old house is gone, there'll be life and love. It was because life and love filled that house that it became a home."

His words comforted me. I know in my heart that when the little plot of land that once held my hollyhock home is plowed over and sown with grain, the sounds of life that once filled the air above it will forever echo through time.

May the circle
be unbroken, By and by
Lord, by and by. There's a
better home awaitin',
In the sky Lord,
in the sky.

Mom 1892-1970

Dad 1891-1969

Todd 1915

Patsie 1936

Pearl 1916

June 1934

Virginia 1917

Billie 1932

Ruby 1918

Johnnie 1931

Opal 1920-1987

Dick 1929-1987

Wilbur 1922

Garnette 1928

Clyde 1925-1977

Afterword/Appreciations

Early one summer morning, Johnnie, Bill, and I carried our coffee cups out to my deck.

"I wonder what ever happened to Slick Blue?" I pondered.

"I don't know," Bill said, "but we sure had fun chasing that poor old tomcat, didn't we?"

"Yes, we sure did," I agreed. "June says that the last time you guys chased him, he jumped from the hay mow and ran limping out across the pasture. She has decided that he just kept running — on across the pasture to the next farm and on and on forever."

Johnnie set his cup on the table and carefully folded his napkin. "I can tell you what happened to him," he stated. "I shot him. I was out hunting and saw him up in that big tree out by the south pond. When I hit him, he fell in the water. It was right before we moved to the farm up by Hull."

"So that's how it ended; that's what happened to old Slick Blue," Bill responded.

"Wasn't that the point of the chase?" Johnny noted.

This early summer morning of reminiscence was one of many I dutifully referred to as "research time" when speaking with my publisher.

All of the surviving Dunker children now live within ten miles of the Pike County farm. The sisters and sisters-in-law get together monthly to talk about new times and old times. The "boys" join us for holidays and other festive occasions. These regular family get-togethers proved invaluable in clearing the fogginess of my childhood memories. Everybody helped. June, Bill, Johnnie, Garnette, Wilbur, Ruby, Virginia, Pearl, and Todd — a special thanks to you and your spouses.

Even though Clyde, Opal, and Dick are gone, the happy years I shared with them have also found their way onto these pages. Writing their chapters has deepened my love and appreciation for each of my departed siblings.

I am proud to say that I am the 13th child of Charles Franklin and Cora Belle Petty Dunker who made our family a circle of strength and love. More than anyone else, they made this book possible.

I cannot forget my children and others who stood by me while I completed the book:

Patrice and Jennifer, who listened again and again to tales they've heard since childhood.

Tommy, who refused to listen — "I'll read it when the book comes out, Mom."

Doug and Steve, my sons-in-law who suffered in silence.

Hannah and Dylan, my adorable grandchildren who didn't suffer in silence. They know that a grandmother's first priority is her grandchildren.

Bonnie Jo, thank you for your dear friendship and your faith in "Aunt Patsie."

Becky Gilligan, you kept my house in order and enjoyed my stories. Thank you.

I am much indebted to the wit and humor of Mark Twain, from whose writings the quotes at the beginning of each chapter are taken. I've often wondered if he ever explored the same islands which "the three little boys" enjoyed.

When Marti Hefley finished reading my first draft, she said, "I loved it. I cried when I read it." Her valued opinion and her chocolate raspberry coffee gave me the courage to wade through the rewrites. Thank you, Marti.

Dr. James Carl Hefley, who believed in me as a writer and with whom I enjoyed comparing "growing-up-in-the-country" stories — thank you. Your book of boyhood recollections, "Way Back in the Hills," served as an inspiration as I struggled to put my own stories on paper.

And one final word of appreciation . . . to my best friend and husband, Marvin J, who endured many a lonely and cold baloney sandwich while I toiled at my computer. We did it Marvin!

The Farm

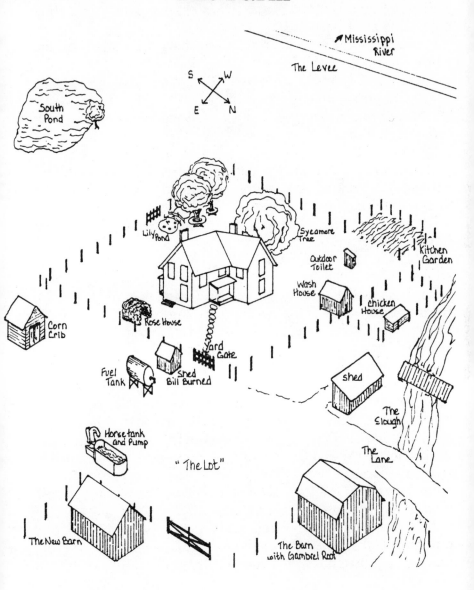

Mom's Recipes

Mom's Homemade Bread

1 quart lukewarm water
2 tablespoons lard
2 tablespoons sugar
1 tablespoon salt
1 cake Fleischman Yeast

Mix. Let stand about ten minutes. Add flour until consistency to handle easy. Knead for a few minutes and let stand covered and rise until light. Make four loaves and let rise until twice in size. Bake.

Mom usually doubled this recipe every other day. Once in awhile she made only six loaves and used the remaining dough for raisin/cinnamon rolls.

Washday Soap

Use granite pans or crocks only.

Any kind of grease (strain to clean if necessary).

To each 5 pounds of lukewarm grease allow 1 can lye and 1 quart cold water.

Mix lye into cold water. Will become hot. Stir once in awhile until gets cold. Pour into grease. Stir until thick and honey colored.

Pour into unchipped granite pans or crocks or wooden box lined with newspaper. Allow to set up.

Every time Mom made this soap, she constantly warned us to keep away when she mixed the lye with water. Once she spilled a pan of the treacherous mixture down the wainscoting side of the sink. It stripped the wood of its many coats of paint and ate a hole in the linoleum. It was enough to make us heed her warnings.

Mom's Molasses-ginger Cookies

1 pint molasses
1 pint white sugar
1 pint lard
2 eggs
2 teaspoons vanilla

Mix together until smooth. Dissolve 1 teaspoon baking soda in 2/3 cup sour milk and set aside.

Mix together:
2 teaspoons baking powder
1/2 teaspoon salt
1 teaspoon cinnamon
3 teaspoons ginger
Pinch of nutmeg
6 cups flour

Add the dry ingredients alternately with milk to shortening mixture. Add additional flour to make dough just firm enough for rolling out on floured board. Don't roll thin. Roll out, sprinkle with white sugar and cut into 2-inch squares. Bake at 300 degrees for approximately 12 minutes. Makes enough 2-inch cookies to fill a two gallon jar.

Mom didn't have a baking time or temperature for these cookies. She baked them until they were just done. Through the years, her daughters determined an oven temperature and an approximate time, but I don't think a one of us, with the exception of Virginia, has ever baked them quite like Mom did. The aroma of these cookies coming out of the oven sure does invite you into the kitchen on a frosty winter day.

ADDITIONAL BOOKS AVAILABLE FROM HANNIBAL BOOKS
Please send me . . . .

12 + Me by Pat Likes. Meet "Pike County Patsie" as she relives her growing-up years on a 300-acre river bottom farm, a stone's throw from the mighty Mississippi. As the youngest of 13 children, Patsie takes you with her as she enjoys the simple pleasures of country living in the late 30's and early 40's. A warm and true family story.

_____ Copies at $7.95 = _____

Way Back in the Hills by James C. Hefley. The story of life "way back in the hills" of the Arkansas Ozarks. Hefley's tale of growing up in this unique culture takes you back to barefoot days in one-room schools, coon hunting half the night, and fishing cold mountain creeks and rivers. This best selling novel brings you to a deeper appreciation of of the simple and good people who have made us what we are.

_____ Copies at $4.95 = _____

Where is God When a Child Suffers? by Penny Geisbrecht. The true story of how a Christian family copes with their child's pain in the light of God's love. You will live through the anguish and questions Jeremy's autism and subsequent burn injury brings to the Giesbrecht family, and then share the answers and peace that God gives them.

_____ Copies at $8.95 = _____

COMING SOON FROM HANNIBAL BOOKS

Way Back When, by James C. Hefley, tells the stories passed down from the real old-timers to Hefl+ey's generation of Ozark hillbilly cousins. You'll read about pioneer settler Sam Davis who discovered his long-lost sister as the wife of the Indian chief who had kidnapped her, "Uncle" Peter escaping from the famous Mountain Meadows Massacre the reformed outlaw who whispered on his death bed that he was the "real" Frank James, brother of Jesse. And much, much more. For release in February, 1990.

_____ Copies at $7.95 = _____

Please add $2.00 postage and handling for first book, plus .50 for each additional book.

Shipping & Handling _____

MO residents add sales tax _____

TOTAL ENCLOSED (Check or money order) _____

Name _____

Address _____

City _____ State _____ Zip _____ Phone _____

Send To: Hannibal Books, 31 Holiday Drive, Hannibal, MO 63401

Gift Giving Made Easy
Send "12 + Me" to a friend.

Simply send us the address of your friend, and a personal message to be included with the book if you wish. Enclose this with your check or money order for $7.95, plus $2 shipping and handling, for each book you'd like sent, and we'll ship "12 + Me" directly to your friend.

Please send **12 + Me** to:

Name _____

Address _____

City _____ State _____ Zip _____ Phone _____

Include the following message: _____

_____

_____

Please send **12 + Me** to:

Name _____

Address _____

City _____ State _____ Zip _____ Phone _____

Include the following message: _____

_____

_____

Total books ordered_____

x $9.95 (7.95 plus $2 shipping)_____

MO residents add sales tax_____

Total amount enclosed_____

Send to: Hannibal Books, 31 Holiday, Hannibal, MO 63401

Book given to Aruilla Smith
By: Lisa Jones. Owner of
The Top of the Mountain Gift Shop,
on No 7 Highway. 2000
Year of 2000.